Nutshell Series
Hornbook Series
and
Black Letter Series
of
WEST PUBLISHING COMPANY
P.O. Box 64526
St. Paul, Minnesota 55164–0526

Accounting

FARIS' ACCOUNTING AND LAW IN A NUTSHELL, 377 pages, 1984. Softcover. (Text)

Administrative Law

GELLHORN AND BOYER'S ADMINISTRATIVE LAW AND PROCESS IN A NUTSHELL, Second Edition, 445 pages, 1981. Softcover. (Text)

Admiralty

MARAIST'S ADMIRALTY IN A NUTSHELL, Second Edition, 379 pages, 1988. Softcover. (Text)

SCHOENBAUM'S HORNBOOK ON ADMIRALTY AND MARITIME LAW, Student Edition, 692 pages, 1987 with 1989 pocket part. (Text)

Agency—Partnership

REUSCHLEIN AND GREGORY'S HORNBOOK ON THE LAW OF AGENCY AND PARTNERSHIP, Second Edition, Approximately 750 pages, October, 1989 Pub. (Text)

STEFFEN'S AGENCY-PARTNERSHIP IN A NUTSHELL, 364 pages, 1977. Softcover. (Text)

American Indian Law

CANBY'S AMERICAN INDIAN LAW IN A NUTSHELL, Second Edition, 336 pages, 1988. Softcover. (Text)

Antitrust—see also Regulated Industries, Trade Regulation

GELLHORN'S ANTITRUST LAW AND ECONOMICS IN A NUTSHELL, Third Edition, 472 pages, 1986. Softcover. (Text)

HOVENKAMP'S BLACK LETTER ON ANTITRUST, 323 pages, 1986. Softcover. (Review)

HOVENKAMP'S HORNBOOK ON ECONOMICS AND FEDERAL ANTITRUST LAW, Student Edition, 414 pages, 1985. (Text)

SULLIVAN'S HORNBOOK OF THE LAW OF ANTITRUST, 886 pages, 1977. (Text)

Appellate Advocacy—see Trial and Appellate Advocacy

Art Law

DUBOFF'S ART LAW IN A NUTSHELL, 335 pages, 1984. Softcover. (Text)

Banking Law

LOVETT'S BANKING AND FINANCIAL INSTITUTIONS LAW IN A NUTSHELL, Second Edition, 464 pages, 1988. Softcover. (Text)

Civil Procedure—see also Federal Jurisdiction and Procedure

CLERMONT'S BLACK LETTER ON CIVIL PROCEDURE, Second Edition, 332 pages, 1988. Softcover. (Review)

FRIEDENTHAL, KANE AND MILLER'S HORNBOOK ON CIVIL PROCEDURE, 876 pages, 1985. (Text)

KANE'S CIVIL PROCEDURE IN A NUTSHELL, Second Edition, 306 pages, 1986. Softcover. (Text)

KOFFLER AND REPPY'S HORNBOOK ON COMMON LAW PLEADING, 663 pages, 1969. (Text)

SIEGEL'S HORNBOOK ON NEW YORK PRACTICE, 1011 pages, 1978, with 1987 pocket part. (Text)

Commercial Law

BAILEY AND HAGEDORN'S SECURED TRANSACTIONS IN A NUTSHELL, Third Edition, 390 pages, 1988. Softcover. (Text)

HENSON'S HORNBOOK ON SECURED TRANSACTIONS UNDER THE U.C.C., Second Edition, 504 pages, 1979, with 1979 pocket part. (Text)

NICKLES' BLACK LETTER ON

Commercial Law—Continued

COMMERCIAL PAPER, 450 pages, 1988. Softcover. (Review)

SPEIDEL'S BLACK LETTER ON SALES AND SALES FINANCING, 363 pages, 1984. Softcover. (Review)

STOCKTON'S SALES IN A NUTSHELL, Second Edition, 370 pages, 1981. Softcover. (Text)

STONE'S UNIFORM COMMERCIAL CODE IN A NUTSHELL, Third Edition, Approximately 540 pages, 1989. Softcover. (Text)

WEBER AND SPEIDEL'S COMMERCIAL PAPER IN A NUTSHELL, Third Edition, 404 pages, 1982. Softcover. (Text)

WHITE AND SUMMERS' HORNBOOK ON THE UNIFORM COMMERCIAL CODE, Third Edition, Student Edition, 1386 pages, 1988. (Text)

Community Property

MENNELL AND BOYKOFF'S COMMUNITY PROPERTY IN A NUTSHELL, Second Edition, 432 pages, 1988. Softcover. (Text)

Comparative Law

GLENDON, GORDON AND OSAKWE'S COMPARATIVE LEGAL TRADITIONS IN A NUTSHELL. 402 pages, 1982. Softcover. (Text)

Conflict of Laws

HAY'S BLACK LETTER ON CONFLICT OF LAWS, Approximately 325 pages, 1989. Softcover. (Review)

SCOLES AND HAY'S HORNBOOK ON CONFLICT OF LAWS, Student Edition, 1085 pages, 1982, with 1989 pocket part. (Text)

SEIGEL'S CONFLICTS IN A NUTSHELL, 470 pages, 1982. Softcover. (Text)

Constitutional Law—Civil Rights

BARRON AND DIENES' BLACK LETTER ON CONSTITUTIONAL LAW, Second Edition, 310 pages, 1987. Softcover. (Review)

BARRON AND DIENES' CONSTITUTIONAL LAW IN A NUTSHELL, 389 pages, 1986. Softcover. (Text)

ENGDAHL'S CONSTITUTIONAL FEDERALISM IN A NUTSHELL, Second Edition, 411 pages, 1987. Softcover. (Text)

MARKS AND COOPER'S STATE CONSTITUTIONAL LAW IN A NUTSHELL, 329 pages, 1988. Softcover. (Text)

Constitutional Law—Civil Rights—Continued

NOWAK, ROTUNDA AND YOUNG'S HORNBOOK ON CONSTITUTIONAL LAW, Third Edition, 1191 pages, 1986 with 1988 pocket part. (Text)

VIEIRA'S CIVIL RIGHTS IN A NUTSHELL, 279 pages, 1978. Softcover. (Text)

WILLIAMS' CONSTITUTIONAL ANALYSIS IN A NUTSHELL, 388 pages, 1979. Softcover. (Text)

Consumer Law—see also Commercial Law

EPSTEIN AND NICKLES' CONSUMER LAW IN A NUTSHELL, Second Edition, 418 pages, 1981. Softcover. (Text)

Contracts

CALAMARI, AND PERILLO'S BLACK LETTER ON CONTRACTS, 397 pages, 1983. Softcover. (Review)

CALAMARI AND PERILLO'S HORNBOOK ON CONTRACTS, Third Edition, 1049 pages, 1987. (Text)

CORBIN'S TEXT ON CONTRACTS, One Volume Student Edition, 1224 pages, 1952. (Text)

FRIEDMAN'S CONTRACT REMEDIES IN A NUTSHELL, 323 pages, 1981. Softcover. (Text)

KEYES' GOVERNMENT CONTRACTS IN A NUTSHELL, 423 pages, 1979. Softcover. (Text)

SCHABER AND ROHWER'S CONTRACTS IN A NUTSHELL, Second Edition, 425 pages, 1984. Softcover. (Text)

Copyright—see Patent and Copyright Law

Corporations

HAMILTON'S BLACK LETTER ON CORPORATIONS, Second Edition, 513 pages, 1986. Softcover. (Review)

HAMILTON'S THE LAW OF CORPORATIONS IN A NUTSHELL, Second Edition, 515 pages, 1987. Softcover. (Text)

HENN AND ALEXANDER'S HORNBOOK ON LAWS OF CORPORATIONS, Third Edition, Student Edition, 1371 pages, 1983, with 1986 pocket part. (Text)

Corrections

KRANTZ' THE LAW OF CORRECTIONS AND PRISONERS' RIGHTS IN A NUTSHELL, Third Edition, 407 pages, 1988. Softcover. (Text)

POPPER'S POST-CONVICTION REMEDIES IN A NUTSHELL, 360 pages, 1978. Softcover.

Corrections—Continued

(Text)

Creditors' Rights

EPSTEIN'S DEBTOR-CREDITOR RELATIONS IN A NUTSHELL, Third Edition, 383 pages, 1986. Softcover. (Text)

NICKLES AND EPSTEIN'S BLACK LETTER ON CREDITORS' RIGHTS AND BANKRUPTCY, 576 pages, 1989. (Review)

Criminal Law and Criminal Procedure—see also Corrections, Juvenile Justice

ISRAEL AND LAFAVE'S CRIMINAL PROCEDURE—CONSTITUTIONAL LIMITATIONS IN A NUTSHELL, Fourth Edition, 461 pages, 1988. Softcover. (Text)

LAFAVE AND ISRAEL'S HORNBOOK ON CRIMINAL PROCEDURE, Student Edition, 1142 pages, 1985, with 1988 pocket part. (Text)

LAFAVE AND SCOTT'S HORNBOOK ON CRIMINAL LAW, Second Edition, 918 pages, 1986. (Text)

LOEWY'S CRIMINAL LAW IN A NUTSHELL, Second Edition, 321 pages, 1987. Softcover. (Text)

LOW'S BLACK LETTER ON CRIMINAL LAW, 433 pages, 1984.

Softcover. (Review)

Decedents' Estates—see Trusts and Estates

Domestic Relations

CLARK'S HORNBOOK ON DOMESTIC RELATIONS, Second Edition, Student Edition, 1050 pages, 1988. (Text)

KRAUSE'S BLACK LETTER ON FAMILY LAW, 314 pages, 1988. Softcover. (Review)

KRAUSE'S FAMILY LAW IN A NUTSHELL, Second Edition, 444 pages, 1986. Softcover. (Text)

Education Law

ALEXANDER AND ALEXANDER'S THE LAW OF SCHOOLS, STUDENTS AND TEACHERS IN A NUTSHELL, 409 pages, 1984. Softcover. (Text)

Employment Discrimination—see also Women and the Law

PLAYER'S FEDERAL LAW OF EMPLOYMENT DISCRIMINATION IN A NUTSHELL, Second Edition, 402 pages, 1981. Softcover. (Text)

PLAYER'S HORNBOOK ON EMPLOYMENT DISCRIMINATION LAW, Student Edition, 708 pages, 1988. (Text)

STUDY AIDS

Energy and Natural Resources Law—see also Oil and Gas

Environmental Law—see also Energy and Natural Resources Law; Sea, Law of

FINDLEY AND FARBER'S ENVIRONMENTAL LAW IN A NUTSHELL, Second Edition, 367 pages, 1988. Softcover. (Text)

RODGERS' HORNBOOK ON ENVIRONMENTAL LAW, 956 pages, 1977, with 1984 pocket part. (Text)

Equity—see Remedies

Estate Planning—see also Trusts and Estates; Taxation—Estate and Gift

LYNN'S AN INTRODUCTION TO ESTATE PLANNING IN A NUTSHELL, Third Edition, 370 pages, 1983. Softcover. (Text)

Evidence

BROUN AND BLAKEY'S BLACK LETTER ON EVIDENCE, 269 pages, 1984. Softcover. (Review)

GRAHAM'S FEDERAL RULES OF EVIDENCE IN A NUTSHELL, Second Edition, 473 pages, 1987. Softcover. (Text)

LILLY'S AN INTRODUCTION TO

THE LAW OF EVIDENCE, Second Edition, 585 pages, 1987. (Text)

MCCORMICK'S HORNBOOK ON EVIDENCE, Third Edition, Student Edition, 1156 pages, 1984, with 1987 pocket part. (Text)

ROTHSTEIN'S EVIDENCE IN A NUTSHELL: STATE AND FEDERAL RULES, Second Edition, 514 pages, 1981. Softcover. (Text)

Federal Jurisdiction and Procedure

CURRIE'S FEDERAL JURISDICTION IN A NUTSHELL, Second Edition, 258 pages, 1981. Softcover. (Text)

REDISH'S BLACK LETTER ON FEDERAL JURISDICTION, 219 pages, 1985. Softcover. (Review)

WRIGHT'S HORNBOOK ON FEDERAL COURTS, Fourth Edition, Student Edition, 870 pages, 1983. (Text)

Future Interests—see Trusts and Estates

Health Law—see Medicine, Law and

Human Rights—see International Law

VI

Immigration Law

WEISSBRODT'S IMMIGRATION LAW AND PROCEDURE IN A NUTSHELL, 345 pages, 1984, Softcover. (Text)

Indian Law—see American Indian Law

Insurance Law

DOBBYN'S INSURANCE LAW IN A NUTSHELL, Second Edition, approximately 285 pages, 1989. Softcover. (Text)

KEETON AND WIDISS' INSURANCE LAW, Student Edition, 1359 pages, 1988. (Text)

International Law—see also Sea, Law of

BUERGENTHAL'S INTERNATIONAL HUMAN RIGHTS IN A NUTSHELL, 283 pages, 1988. Softcover. (Text)

BUERGENTHAL AND MAIER'S PUBLIC INTERNATIONAL LAW IN A NUTSHELL, 262 pages, 1985. Softcover. (Text)

FOLSOM, GORDON AND SPANOGLE'S INTERNATIONAL BUSINESS TRANSACTIONS IN A NUTSHELL, Third Edition, 509 pages, 1988. Softcover. (Text)

Interviewing and Counseling

SHAFFER AND ELKINS' LEGAL INTERVIEWING AND COUNSELING IN A NUTSHELL, Second Edition, 487 pages, 1987. Softcover. (Text)

Introduction to Law—see Legal Method and Legal System

Introduction to Law Study

HEGLAND'S INTRODUCTION TO THE STUDY AND PRACTICE OF LAW IN A NUTSHELL, 418 pages, 1983. Softcover (Text)

KINYON'S INTRODUCTION TO LAW STUDY AND LAW EXAMINATIONS IN A NUTSHELL, 389 pages, 1971. Softcover. (Text)

Juvenile Justice

FOX'S JUVENILE COURTS IN A NUTSHELL, Third Edition, 291 pages, 1984. Softcover. (Text)

Labor Law—see also Employment Discrimination, Social Legislation

LESLIE'S LABOR LAW IN A NUTSHELL, Second Edition, 397 pages, 1986. Softcover. (Text)

NOLAN'S LABOR ARBITRATION LAW AND PRACTICE IN A NUTSHELL, 358 pages, 1979. Softcover. (Text)

STUDY AIDS

Land Finance—Property Security—see Real Estate Transactions

Land Use

HAGMAN AND JUERGENSMEYER'S HORNBOOK ON URBAN PLANNING AND LAND DEVELOPMENT CONTROL LAW, Second Edition, Student Edition, 680 pages, 1986. (Text)

WRIGHT AND WRIGHT'S LAND USE IN A NUTSHELL, Second Edition, 356 pages, 1985. Softcover. (Text)

Legal Method and Legal System—see also Legal Research, Legal Writing

KEMPIN'S HISTORICAL INTRODUCTION TO ANGLO-AMERICAN LAW IN A NUTSHELL, Second Edition, 280 pages, 1973. Softcover. (Text)

REYNOLDS' JUDICIAL PROCESS IN A NUTSHELL, 292 pages, 1980. Softcover. (Text)

Legal Research

COHEN'S LEGAL RESEARCH IN A NUTSHELL, Fourth Edition, 452 pages, 1985. Softcover. (Text)

Legal Writing

SQUIRES AND ROMBAUER'S LEGAL WRITING IN A NUTSHELL, 294 pages, 1982. Softcover. (Text)

Legislation

DAVIES' LEGISLATIVE LAW AND PROCESS IN A NUTSHELL, Second Edition, 346 pages, 1986. Softcover. (Text)

Local Government

MCCARTHY'S LOCAL GOVERNMENT LAW IN A NUTSHELL, Second Edition, 404 pages, 1983. Softcover. (Text)

REYNOLDS' HORNBOOK ON LOCAL GOVERNMENT LAW, 860 pages, 1982, with 1987 pocket part. (Text)

Mass Communication Law

ZUCKMAN, GAYNES, CARTER AND DEE'S MASS COMMUNICATIONS LAW IN A NUTSHELL, Third Edition, 538 pages, 1988. Softcover. (Text)

Medicine, Law and

KING'S THE LAW OF MEDICAL MALPRACTICE IN A NUTSHELL, Second Edition, 342 pages, 1986. Softcover. (Text)

Military Law

SHANOR AND TERRELL'S MILITARY LAW IN A NUTSHELL, 378 pages, 1980. Softcover. (Text)

Mortgages—see Real Estate Transactions

Natural Resources Law—see Energy and Natural Resources Law, Environmental Law

Office Practice—see also Interviewing and Counseling

HEGLAND'S TRIAL AND PRACTICE SKILLS IN A NUTSHELL, 346 pages, 1978. Softcover (Text)

Oil and Gas

HEMINGWAY'S HORNBOOK ON OIL AND GAS, Second Edition, Student Edition, 543 pages, 1983, with 1989 pocket part. (Text)

LOWE'S OIL AND GAS LAW IN A NUTSHELL, Second Edition, 465 pages, 1988. Softcover. (Text)

Partnership—see Agency— Partnership

Patent and Copyright Law

MILLER AND DAVIS' INTELLECTUAL PROPERTY—PATENTS, TRADEMARKS AND COPYRIGHT IN A NUTSHELL, 428 pages, 1983. Softcover. (Text)

Products Liability

PHILLIPS' PRODUCTS LIABILITY IN A NUTSHELL, Third Edition,

307 pages, 1988. Softcover. (Text)

Professional Responsibility

ARONSON AND WECKSTEIN'S PROFESSIONAL RESPONSIBILITY IN A NUTSHELL, 399 pages, 1980. Softcover. (Text)

ROTUNDA'S BLACK LETTER ON PROFESSIONAL RESPONSIBILITY, Second Edition, 414 pages, 1988. Softcover. (Review)

WOLFRAM'S HORNBOOK ON MODERN LEGAL ETHICS, Student Edition, 1120 pages, 1986. (Text)

Property—see also Real Estate Transactions, Land Use, Trusts and Estates

BERNHARDT'S BLACK LETTER ON PROPERTY, 318 pages, 1983. Softcover. (Review)

BERNHARDT'S REAL PROPERTY IN A NUTSHELL, Second Edition, 448 pages, 1981. Softcover. (Text)

BURKE'S PERSONAL PROPERTY IN A NUTSHELL, 322 pages, 1983. Softcover. (Text)

CUNNINGHAM, STOEBUCK AND WHITMAN'S HORNBOOK ON THE LAW OF PROPERTY, Student Edition, 916 pages, 1984, with 1987 pocket part. (Text)

HILL'S LANDLORD AND TENANT

Property—Continued

LAW IN A NUTSHELL, Second Edition, 311 pages, 1986. Softcover. (Text)

Real Estate Transactions

BRUCE'S REAL ESTATE FINANCE IN A NUTSHELL, Second Edition, 262 pages, 1985. Softcover. (Text)

NELSON AND WHITMAN'S BLACK LETTER ON LAND TRANSACTIONS AND FINANCE, Second Edition, 466 pages, 1988. Softcover. (Review)

NELSON AND WHITMAN'S HORNBOOK ON REAL ESTATE FINANCE LAW, Second Edition, 941 pages, 1985 with 1989 pocket part. (Text)

Regulated Industries—see also Mass Communication Law, Banking Law

GELLHORN AND PIERCE'S REGULATED INDUSTRIES IN A NUTSHELL, Second Edition, 389 pages, 1987. Softcover. (Text)

Remedies

DOBBS' HORNBOOK ON REMEDIES, 1067 pages, 1973. (Text)

DOBBYN'S INJUNCTIONS IN A NUTSHELL, 264 pages, 1974. Softcover. (Text)

FRIEDMAN'S CONTRACT REMEDIES IN A NUTSHELL, 323 pages, 1981. Softcover. (Text)

MCCORMICK'S HORNBOOK ON DAMAGES, 811 pages, 1935. (Text)

O'CONNELL'S REMEDIES IN A NUTSHELL, Second Edition, 320 pages, 1985. Softcover. (Text)

Sea, Law of

SOHN AND GUSTAFSON'S THE LAW OF THE SEA IN A NUTSHELL, 264 pages, 1984. Softcover. (Text)

Securities Regulation

HAZEN'S HORNBOOK ON THE LAW OF SECURITIES REGULATION, Student Edition, 739 pages, 1985, with 1988 pocket part. (Text)

RATNER'S SECURITIES REGULATION IN A NUTSHELL, Third Edition, 316 pages, 1988. Softcover. (Text)

Social Legislation

HOOD AND HARDY'S WORKERS' COMPENSATION AND EMPLOYEE PROTECTION IN A NUTSHELL, 274 pages, 1984. Softcover. (Text)

LAFRANCE'S WELFARE LAW: STRUCTURE AND ENTITLEMENT IN A NUTSHELL, 455 pages, 1979. Softcover. (Text)

Sports Law

SCHUBERT, SMITH AND TRENTADUE'S SPORTS LAW, 395 pages, 1986. (Text)

Taxation—Corporate

WEIDENBRUCH AND BURKE'S FEDERAL INCOME TAXATION OF CORPORATIONS AND STOCKHOLDERS IN A NUTSHELL, Third Edition, 309 pages, 1989. Softcover. (Text)

Taxation—Estate & Gift—see also Estate Planning, Trusts and Estates

MCNULTY'S FEDERAL ESTATE AND GIFT TAXATION IN A NUTSHELL, Fourth Edition, 496 pages, 1989. Softcover. (Text)

Taxation—Individual

HUDSON AND LIND'S BLACK LETTER ON FEDERAL INCOME TAXATION, Second Edition, 396 pages, 1987. Softcover. (Review)

MCNULTY'S FEDERAL INCOME TAXATION OF INDIVIDUALS IN A NUTSHELL, Fourth Edition, 503 pages, 1988. Softcover. (Text)

POSIN'S HORNBOOK ON FEDERAL INCOME TAXATION, Student Edition, 491 pages, 1983, with 1989 pocket part. (Text)

ROSE AND CHOMMIE'S HORNBOOK ON FEDERAL INCOME TAXATION, Third Edition, 923 pages, 1988, with 1989 pocket part. (Text)

Taxation—International

DOERNBERG'S INTERNATIONAL TAXATION IN A NUTSHELL, 325 pages, 1989. Softcover. (Text)

Taxation—State & Local

GELFAND AND SALSICH'S STATE AND LOCAL TAXATION AND FINANCE IN A NUTSHELL, 309 pages, 1986. Softcover. (Text)

Torts—see also Products Liability

KIONKA'S BLACK LETTER ON TORTS, 339 pages, 1988. Softcover. (Review)

KIONKA'S TORTS IN A NUTSHELL: INJURIES TO PERSONS AND PROPERTY, 434 pages, 1977. Softcover. (Text)

MALONE'S TORTS IN A NUTSHELL: INJURIES TO FAMILY, SOCIAL AND TRADE RELATIONS, 358 pages, 1979. Softcover. (Text)

PROSSER AND KEETON'S HORNBOOK ON TORTS, Fifth Edition, Student Edition, 1286 pages, 1984 with 1988 pocket part.

Water Law—see also Environmental Law

GETCHES' WATER LAW IN A NUTSHELL, 439 pages, 1984. Softcover. (Text)

Wills—see Trusts and Estates

Women and the Law—see also Employment Discrimination

THOMAS' SEX DISCRIMINATION IN A NUTSHELL, 399 pages, 1982. Softcover. (Text)

Workers' Compensation—see Social Legislation

Advisory Board

XIV

PUBLIC INTERNATIONAL LAW

IN A NUTSHELL

SECOND EDITION

By

THOMAS BUERGENTHAL
Lobingier Professor of
Comparative and International Law
George Washington University Law School
Judge, Inter–American Court
of Human Rights

HAROLD G. MAIER
David Daniels Allen
Professor of Law
and
Director of Transnational Legal Studies
Vanderbilt Law School

ST. PAUL, MINN.
WEST PUBLISHING CO.
1990

COPYRIGHT © 1985 By WEST PUBLISHING CO.
COPYRIGHT © 1990 By WEST PUBLISHING CO.
50 West Kellogg Boulevard
P.O. Box 64526
St. Paul, MN 55164–0526

Library of Congress Cataloging-in-Publication Data

Buergenthal, Thomas.
    Public international law in a nutshell / by Thomas Buergenthal,
Harold G. Maier. — 2nd ed.
        p.   cm. — (Nutshell series)
    ISBN 0–314–66371–1
    1. International law. I. Maier, Harold G., 1937–   . II. Title. III.
Series.
JX3091.B84   1989
341—dc20

89–22720
CIP

ISBN 0–314–66371–1

PREFACE TO THE SECOND EDITION

This second edition of the Nutshell on Public International Law is organized in accordance with the same general principles described in the Preface to the First Edition. The authors have updated and expanded the treatment of various sections of the earlier work. In this effort we have been aided by much constructive criticism from our colleagues in the field. While space does not permit mentioning all who made useful suggestions, we found criticism and comments by Professors Homer Angelo, Richard Graving and Edith Brown Weiss to be especially helpful. Any errors or omissions that may remain are, of course, the responsibility of the authors alone.

THOMAS BUERGENTHAL
HAROLD G. MAIER

September 1989

*

PREFACE TO THE
FIRST EDITION

This book was written to serve a dual purpose. It is designed to introduce the lawyer and law student to the basic doctrines, institutions and methodology of modern public international law. It is also intended as a text capable of supplementing and helping with the conceptual integration of the teaching materials on international law in use in the United States. Although *Nutshells* usually perform only the latter function, the absence of an up-to-date American international law monograph, written for lawyers, accounts for this attempt to fill the gap, albeit only in a small way, with a text providing an overview of the subject and signposts for additional research.

In a short book of this type, the risk is great that in the effort to consolidate and to be brief, material will be distorted or oversimplified. To reduce the risk—one can probably never escape it totally—we opted not to discuss various highly specialized subjects and certain emerging areas of international law, thereby gaining more space to cover the basic material in somewhat greater detail. We do not discuss the law of the sea, for example, in part because a recently published *Nut-*

shell on the Law of the Sea (1984), by Louis B. Sohn and Kristen Gustafson, covers that subject expertly and concisely. Neither do we treat international economic law or international environmental law, nor do we explore the complexities of the law applicable to the use of force in modern international law, to mention but a few of the more obvious omissions.

What to cover and what to omit is ultimately, of course, a matter of personal judgment and preference as well as of available space. Our decision regarding content and coverage was guided in part by what we deem to be important for an understanding of the basic elements of modern international law, recognizing full well that much more remains to be said about the topics we have covered and that a great deal of material has not been considered at all. We hope that this book will stimulate the reader to pursue the further study of international law. It is a fascinating subject well worth the intellectual effort. Given the world we live in, moreover, it is a subject whose basic institutions and concepts need to be understood by the legal profession as a whole.

THOMAS BUERGENTHAL
HAROLD G. MAIER

June 1985

ACKNOWLEDGMENTS

The authors would like to express their profound appreciation to their student research assistants for the many valuable contributions they made to this book. Professor Maier wishes to acknowledge the research assistance of William A. Zan Blue, Nancie L. Combs, Charles R. Mandly, Jr., Susan D. Romer, Michael J. Russell and Tia Wolfson Barancik, who assisted with the first edition, Michele Behaylo who assisted with this edition, all at Vanderbilt Law School, and to thank Howard Hood, Esq., Associate Director of the Vanderbilt Law Library. Professor Buergenthal owes a special debt of gratitude to Susan Borecki and Philip Weintraub, his research assistants at the Washington College of Law of the American University who assisted with the first edition, and to Martin Aversa and Joseph Perna, his research assistants at the George Washington University Law School, who worked with him on the second edition.

Funds to assist with the research and writing of this book were contributed by the Vanderbilt Law School and the George Washington University Law School. This assistance is gratefully acknowledged by both authors.

ACKNOWLEDGMENTS

Professor Buergenthal also wishes to express his special appreciation to his wife, Marjorie J. (Peggy) Buergenthal for her understanding, help and support, which contributed immensely to the publication of this book.

THOMAS BUERGENTHAL
HAROLD G. MAIER

September 1989

OUTLINE

Chapter 1. The Application and Relevance of International Law

Chapter 5. The International Law of Treaties

Chapter 6. The Rights of Individuals

A. The Law of the UN Charter

Chapter 8. Foreign Relations Law in the United States

Chapter 9. Immunities

(B. & M.) Public Int'l Law, 2nd Ed. NS—2

Chapter 10.   International Legal Research Sources

TABLE OF CASES

References are to Pages

TABLE OF CASES

PUBLIC INTERNATIONAL LAW

IN A NUTSHELL

SECOND EDITION

CHAPTER 1

THE APPLICATION AND RELEVANCE OF INTERNATIONAL LAW

I. INTRODUCTION

This chapter introduces the reader to the basic concepts of modern public international law and provides an overview of the historical and theoretical context within which that law has developed. Also discussed are the so-called subjects of international law as well as the function international law performs and its application on the domestic and on the international plane.

II. PROBLEMS OF DEFINITION

§ 1–1. **The traditional definition.** International law used to be defined as the law that governs relations between states. Under the traditional definition, only states were subjects of international law, that is, only states were deemed to have rights and obligations that international law recognized. Whatever benefits or burdens international law conferred or imposed on other entities or individuals were considered to be purely derivative, flowing to these so-called "objects" of international law by virtue of their relations to or dependence upon a state.

1

§ 1–2. States under international law.
When international lawyers speak of states, they
mean sovereign or nation-states. To qualify as a
state under international law, an entity must have
a territory, a population, a government and the
capacity to engage in diplomatic or foreign relations. States in federal unions, provinces or can-
tons usually lack the last attribute, which is a vital
element of sovereignty. See generally, 1 Oppenheim's International Law: A Treatise 118–19 (H.
Lauterpacht, 8th ed. 1955.).

§ 1–3. Modern definition. Contemporary international law, although still considered to be
principally the law governing relations between
states, is no longer deemed to be exclusively limited to those relations. It has a wide reach and is
more properly defined as law that deals "with the
conduct of states and of international organizations
and with their relations *inter se*, as well as with
some of their relations with persons, whether natural or juridical." ALI, Restatement of the Foreign
Relations Law of the United States (Third) (hereinafter referred to as "Restatement (Third)"), § 101
(1987).

§ 1–4. Modern subjects. Today intergovernmental international organizations, see Chapter 3,
infra, and even individuals, albeit to a much more
limited extent, are and can be the subjects of rights
and obligations under international law. The
United Nations, for example, enjoys the legal capacity to enter into treaty relations, governed by

and binding under international law, with states and other international organizations. See Advisory Opinion on Reparations for Injuries Suffered in the Service of the United Nations, 1949 ICJ 3. The direct responsibility of individuals for war crimes and the development of the international law on human rights indicates furthermore that, in certain circumstances, individuals may have rights and obligations under international law that are not derivative in the traditional sense. See Chapter 6, infra.

III. INTERNATIONAL AND DOMESTIC APPLICATION

§ 1–5. **Application distinguished.** The fact that international law, for the most part, governs inter-state relations does not mean that it is irrelevant on the domestic legal plane or that it is not applied there. The manner in which international law is applied on the domestic and on the international plane differs, however, even though the rules as such may be the same. When studying international law, it is useful, therefore, to be aware of these differences between the domestic and the international application of international law.

§ 1–6. **International application.** On the international plane, international law is invoked and applied on a daily basis by states and by intergovernmental organizations. With minor exceptions, it is the only law that applies to the conduct of states and international organizations in their relations with one another. Here international law is a distinct legal system, comparable in its scope and function to a domestic legal system.

§ 1–7. **Domestic application.** On the domestic plane, international law is not a legal system. When we say in the U.S., for example, that international law is "the law of the land," we are in fact saying that it is a branch of our legal system, in very much the same way that the law of torts or contracts is a branch of our legal system. We refer to the American law of torts in a case or situation involving issues that can be characterized as being governed by principles of tort law. In much the same way, we refer to international law when the facts of the case or situation demand it. Here international law is invoked in domestic litigation and other contexts by individuals, private and public entities, and government agencies whenever resort to it appears to be relevant. The question whether the individual invoking international law in an American court, for example, has rights or obligations under international law on the international plane, that is, whether he/she is a subject of international law, is for the most part irrelevant. The relevant question here is whether this or that rule of international law is, as a matter of American law, appropriate to the resolution of the controversy before the court. Viewed from this domestic perspective, the individual is the subject of rights and obligations which have their source in international law to the same extent that the individual is the subject of domestic legal rights and obligations.

§ 1–8. The international and domestic application: some examples. Let us assume that international law requires states in peacetime to grant foreign merchant ships free passage through their territorial waters. Let us assume further that a merchant ship flying the flag of State X and belonging to Mr. Barco, a national of State X, is seized by the coast guard of State Y in its territorial waters in violation of the above mentioned international law rule. On the international plane, the resulting dispute would be between State X and State Y. This would be so because the right to free passage by merchant ships and the obligation to comply with it are rights and obligations appertaining only to the subjects of international law— the states. The seizure of Mr. Barco's ship would be deemed to be a breach of an obligation owed by State Y to State X, the state of the ship's nationality. That nationality entitles State X to assert a claim against State Y. Under general international law, an injury to a state's national is deemed to be an injury to the state. Mavrommatis Palestine Concessions (Jurisdiction), 1924 PCIJ, ser. A, No. 2.

Now let us assume that instead of proceeding through State X in the manner indicated above, Mr. Barco files a suit in the courts of State Y, seeking both the release of his ship and damages. If international law is the law of the land in State

Y, which it is in different guises in most, if not all, states comprising the community of nations, Mr. Barco would have the right to invoke the relevant rule of international law to assert the illegality of the seizure of his ship. Here he would claim the violation of a right enjoyed by him under international law in much the same way that he would rely on a rule of the domestic law of torts or property if someone had deprived him of the use of his property in a business transaction in State Y. Whether the case concerns the law of torts or property or international law, its outcome in State Y will depend upon the legal and factual soundness of the claim under the relevant domestic law, both substantive and procedural, of State Y.

On the international plane, the context for the application of the international law rule relating to free passage of ships through territorial waters in peacetime is the international legal system. That is to say, here all issues bearing on the case, for example, whether the rule takes precedence or not over other rules, etc., would be determined by international law. On the domestic plane, the context for the application of the rule is the domestic legal system and constitutional framework. And while it is true, as a general proposition, that a domestic court would seek to determine the content of a rule of international law in much the same way as an international court, the same controversy might well be resolved differently by each of them because in one case the judicial context is the domestic legal system and in the other it is the international legal system. That is why it is so important, when dealing with international law questions and materials, to inquire whether the context is the domestic or international plane, or both.

§ 1–9. **The supremacy of international law.** The rights and obligations which a state has under international law are, on the international plane, superior to any rights or duties it may have under its domestic law. Thus, for example, if a state is a party to a treaty that is valid and binding under international law, its non-performance cannot be excused as a matter of international law on the ground that the treaty was declared unconstitutional by its supreme court. With minor exceptions not here relevant, the unconstitutionality of the treaty is a purely domestic law issue. See Vienna Convention on the Law of Treaties, arts. 27 and 46. Although it might prevent the state from giving effect to the treaty, its failure to perform would nevertheless constitute a breach of international law. In practice, this type of problem tends to be resolved by renegotiation of the treaty or, in rare instances, by the payment of compensation.

Conceptually, the inability of a state for domestic constitutional reasons to perform a treaty obligation valid under international law resembles domestic situations in which one party to a contract is unable or unwilling to comply with its contractual obligations and is liable for the consequences of its breach. Moreover, whether the decision of a state not to comply with a treaty is compelled by its supreme court or by a decision of its president, for example, is equally irrelevant under international law. Domestic constitutional law does not on the international plane supersede international law, even though such constitutional law may, and usually does in most countries, take precedence over international law on the domestic plane.

IV. RELEVANCE AND FUNCTION OF INTERNATIONAL LAW

§ 1–10. **The uses of international law.** International law is routinely applied by international tribunals as well as by domestic courts. But international law is not relevant solely in judicial proceedings. States rely on it in their diplomatic relations, in their negotiations, and in their policymaking. States defend their actions and policies by reference to international law and challenge the conduct of other states in reliance on it. To the extent that international law is perceived as "law" by the international community, to that extent it imposes restraints on the behavior of states and affects their decision-making process. Although there may be considerable disagreement in a particular case about the nature, scope or applicability of a given rule of international law, states rarely admit to violating international law and hardly ever assert the right to do so.

§ **1–11. International law as law.** The conduct of states is conditioned by many factors; international law is only one of them. Sometimes it is determinative, many times it is not. Yet whoever seeks to understand or predict how states will act in a given situation, or whoever has to counsel states on how they should act consistent with their national self-interest, needs to take applicable principles of international law into account. A state may be prepared to violate international law in order to achieve a given political objective. But in calculating the short- and long-term political costs of such action, the state's policymakers will have to address questions relating to the nature and function of that law as well as the legal and political consequences of being labeled a law-breaker.

The dramatic violations of international law, principally those involving the threat or use of force, which attract worldwide attention, should not blind us to the fact that the vast body of international law which regulates international commerce, communication, transportation, and day-to-day diplomatic and consular relations, to mention but a few areas, is applied and observed as routinely as is domestic law. For lawyers working in these fields, whether as legal advisers to governments, to international organizations or to corporations, or as legislators, policymakers, or arbitrators, international law is law in a very real, practical sense. They have to know how to find and analyze it, in what context to apply it, where and how to enforce it.

§ 1–12. Application and enforcement. Questions about enforcement arise the moment international law is mentioned. In addressing these questions, it is important to ask whether we are talking about enforcement on the domestic or on the international plane. On the domestic plane, international law tends to be enforced by courts and administrative agencies in much the same manner as any other domestic law. The answer is more complex when we turn to the international plane.

As a rule, international courts do not have compulsory or automatic jurisdiction to deal with all international legal disputes that might be ripe for adjudication. The authority of these courts to hear a given dispute depends upon the acceptance of their jurisdiction by the parties to the dispute. See Chapter 4, infra. There are, as a consequence, many international legal disputes that cannot be adjudicated because one or the other of the parties to the dispute refuses to accept the jurisdiction of a court.

But courts are not the only institutions for the resolution of disputes between states. Many international disputes that cannot be submitted to formal international adjudication, can and have been settled by other methods such as negotiation, mediation, good offices or arbitration, which all involve the application of international law. See Chapter 4, infra. Here international law performs a function similar to that which domestic law performs in the settlement of disputes that do not reach the courts.

Furthermore, numerous methods and organizations exist today, whether of a political, quasi-judicial, or diplomatic character—the United Nations, regional organizations, diplomatic conferences, multilateral commissions, etc.—where international law plays a role, together with other factors, in resolving conflicts and in fashioning solutions to societal problems of all types. Law plays a comparable role on the domestic plane. Here too, as on the international plane, its impact outside the formal judicial setting may, at different times and in different contexts, be of marginal significance, quite important or determinative in shaping political compromises or dealing with the problems confronting a given society.

§ 1–13. **Enforcement and compliance.** The mechanisms available on the international plane for the enforcement of a judgment rendered by international courts differ from those that may be available on the domestic plane. See Chapter 4, infra. International tribunals do not have a sheriff or police force who can be ordered to enforce a judgment. But even on the domestic plane, judgments are enforced or executed differently depending upon whether the judgment was rendered against a private party or against the government. While the property of private parties may be attached to execute judgments against them, such a

remedy is usually not available against governmental entities. The enforcement powers of domestic courts, furthermore, are more symbolic
than real when the confrontation is between them
and the government. Governments comply with
domestic court decisions not because the courts
have the actual police or military power to force
compliance. The extent of compliance tends, rather, to be a function of the political legitimacy and
moral credibility that sustain the entire fabric of
governmental authority and produce the expectation that law will be obeyed.

The situation is not all that different on the
international plane. It is true, nevertheless, that
the absence of a formal centralized lawmaking
authority, coupled with the debilitating jurisdictional defects of international courts, weaken the
expectation of compliance in comparison with the
situation that exists on the domestic plane. These
considerations need to be balanced against the risk
that non-complying governments open themselves
up to costly retaliatory measures by other governments. The likelihood of such retaliation, whether
it be political or economic, is an element that has
an important impact on compliance by states with
their international obligations. Moreover, even
the strongest states have long-term and short-term
political and economic interests in an international
order in which conflicts are resolved in accordance
with generally accepted rules, in a manner that is

reasonably predictable, and that reduces the likelihood of resort to force.

V. HISTORICAL OVERVIEW

§ 1-14. The origins of the modern system. International law or the law of nations, as it used to be called, came into its own as a separate legal system or discipline with the emergence of the modern nation-state in the sixteenth and seventeenth centuries. Of course, practices such as the exchange of diplomatic emissaries, the conclusion of peace treaties, etc., and some of the rules applicable to them can be traced back far into antiquity. But it was not until modern times that the rules governing relations between states came to be seen as a distinct body of law. Many of these rules were derived either from Roman law or Canon law, which drew heavily on principles of natural law. These two sources of law also formed the basis of much of the domestic law of the nation-states that came into being in Europe as the Medieval period drew to a close with the dawn of the Renaissance. Roman law and Canon law exerted great influence on the European statesmen and legal scholars of the period who created and systematized what became modern international law. See generally, Nussbaum, A Concise History of the Law of Nations (rev. ed. 1962).

§ 1-15. Major early writers and theories. Hugo Grotius (1583–1645), a Dutch scholar and diplomat, is known as the "father" of modern international law. His major work, *De Jure Belli Ac Pacis* (1625), is one of the earliest attempts to provide a systematic overview of the international law of war and peace. Among Grotius' other important works is *Mare Liberum* (1609), a forceful brief on behalf of the doctrine of freedom of the seas, which in due course came to be accepted as a basic principle of international law.

Grotius was preceded by a number of writers whose important contributions to the development of international law should be noted. Leading among these are the Italian Alberico Gentili (1552–1608), a professor of Roman law at Oxford University, who wrote *De Jure Belli* (1598), and the Spanish theologian, Francisco de Vitoria (1480–1546), who, in his lectures on the Spanish conquests in the New World, was among the first to assert the universal character and applicability of international law.

Of importance among the early writers on international law who followed Grotius is the German scholar, Samuel Pufendorf (1632–1694). In his *De Jure Naturae Gentium* (1672), Pufendorf espoused the view that natural law was the source or basis of international law. An individual whose influence rivaled that of Grotius for a considerable period of time was the Swiss diplomat, Emmerich de Vattel (1714–1767). His principal work, *The Law of Nations* (1758), a practical guide to international law for diplomats, was widely cited and relied upon by governments even in the late 19th century.

While Pufendorf and Vattel advanced the view that natural law was the true source of international law, the English legal scholar, Richard Zouche (1590–1660), was one of the early positivists. Partisans of positivism looked to state practice as the source of international law, seeking the basis of this law in the consent of the states— its subjects. Both schools of thought found some support in Grotius' writings, because his theories about international law relied on natural law and on custom established by the practice of states. These two schools dominated the philosophical discourse about the nature of international law into the early decades of the 20th century. Positivism gradually emerged as the dominant theory, leading to the acceptance of the view that international law as law depended upon the sovereign consent of the states comprising the international community. The requisite consent had to be sought in the practice of states deemed by them to have the force of law. See Chapter 2, § 2–3, infra.

§ 1–16. Historical milestones. A number of events or historical milestones mark the development of modern international law. Among these are the Peace of Westphalia, the Congress of Vienna, the establishment of the League of Nations and the adoption of the Charter of the United Nations.

The Peace of Westphalia ended the Thirty Years' War (1618–1648) and established a treaty-based system or framework for peace and cooperation in Europe, which endured for more than a hundred years. It provided, *inter alia,* for the coexistence in certain parts of Europe of Catholicism and Protestantism, thus planting early seeds of religious freedom in Europe. The foundations for multi-state diplomatic congresses and negotiations were laid at the conferences that produced the two basic treaties comprising the Peace of Westphalia. These agreements also proclaimed the doctrine of *pacta sunt servanda* (treaties are to be observed) and established a machinery for the settlement of disputes arising between the signatories.

The Final Act of the Congress of Vienna (1815) formally ended the Napoleonic Wars and fashioned a sophisticated multilateral system of political and economic cooperation in Europe. The major aspects of this system survived until the outbreak of the First World War. The Congress adopted the first comprehensive set of rules governing diplomatic protocol, it formally condemned the slave trade, and it established the principle of free and unimpeded navigation on international rivers traversing the region. The Congress laid the foundation for the recognition of the neutrality of Switzerland and its guarantee by the principal European powers. Attached to the Final Act, furthermore, were various multilateral and bilateral agreements which, together with the treaties that emerged from and followed upon the Peace of Westphalia, provided Europe with a substantial body of international law and contributed in a very significant manner to the development of modern international law.

The League of Nations came into being in 1920 with the entry into force of its Covenant. The Covenant formed an integral part of the Treaty of Versailles, which ended World War I. Although the failure of the League of Nations to prevent World War II is a well-known historical fact, it is important to remember that this organization con- stituted the first serious effort by states to create a permanent inter-governmental institutional frame- work for the resolution of political disputes and the preservation of peace. It was the League that established the Permanent Court of International Justice, the first such international tribunal open to all states. The machinery created by the League for the protection of the rights of minori- ties in eastern and southeastern Europe and for the supervision of certain non-selfgoverning terri- tories (Mandates) constituted the first internation- al attempt to establish international institutions for the protection of human rights. The League contributed in numerous other ways to the devel- opment and codification of international law. Moreover, the modern law of international organi- zations, see Chapter 3, infra, came into being with the establishment of the League of Nations and the legal precedents it set.

The United Nations, which was founded in 1945, is discussed in detail in Chapter 3, infra. Here it

needs to be emphasized only that the mere existence of the UN, whatever its weaknesses, constitutes a further advance in the efforts of the international community to make international law a
more effective tool for the preservation of international peace and the improvement of the human
condition throughout the world. The UN's legal
and political achievements, if measured by the job
that remains to be done, are limited at best; if
they are judged in relation to the accomplishments
of the international law and organizations that
preceded the UN, its contributions gain greatly in
significance. Whether international law and organizations can in today's world make a truly significant contribution to the solution of the problems
facing mankind remains the most critical issue for
international lawyers everywhere. It should be
the fundamental theme that animates and perme-
ates the study of international law.

CHAPTER 2

THE SOURCES OF
INTERNATIONAL LAW

I. INTRODUCTION

The formal sources of domestic law are the constitution, if a country has one, legislative enactments and, where the doctrine of binding precedent (*stare decisis*) prevails, decisions of judicial tribunals (caselaw). Thus, if an American lawyer, for example, were to be asked, "how do you know that this rule is the law?", he or she would point to one of these sources. Another way of looking at sources of law is to ask, "how is law made?" The answer, on the domestic plane, is to point to the constitutional, legislative, or judicial process from which law emanates.

The situation is more complicated on the international plane. Viewed in terms of law-making, international law is a primitive legal system. Here there exists no institution that is comparable to a national legislature with power to promulgate laws of general applicability. The international community lacks a constitution that can be viewed as a fundamental source of law. Moreover, decisions of the International Court of Justice are legally binding only on the parties to the dispute and have no precedential value in a formal sense because *stare decisis* is not a rule of international law.

How then do we know whether a given rule is international law? This question can be answered only by reference to the sources of international law and by analyzing the manner in which international law is made or how it becomes law binding on the international plane. This chapter deals with this question as well as with issues relating to the manner in which the existence or non-existence of a rule of international law may be proved.

II. PRIMARY SOURCES

§ 2–1. Article 38(1) of the Statute of the International Court of Justice. This provision is generally considered to be the most authoritative enumeration of the sources of international law. It reads as follows:

The Court, whose function is to decide in accordance with international law such disputes as are submitted to it, shall apply:

a. international conventions, whether general or particular, establishing rules expressly recognized by the contesting states;

b. international custom, as evidence of a general practice accepted as law;

c. the general principles of law recognized by civilized nations;

d.   . . . judicial decisions and the teachings of the most highly qualified publicists of the various nations, as subsidiary means for the determination of rules of law.

§ 2–2. Meaning of Article 38 of the ICJ Statute. Article 38 was included in the Statute of the ICJ to describe the nature of the international law that the Court was to apply. (The ICJ is discussed in Chapter 4, infra.) Article 38(1) indicates that international law consists of or has its basis in international conventions (treaties), international custom, and general principles of law. It follows that a rule cannot be deemed to be international law unless it is derived from one of these three sources. This is also the view that the new Restatement adopts. Restatement (Third) § 102(1).

"Judicial decisions" and the "teachings" of the publicists are not sources of law as such; they are "subsidiary means" for finding what the law is. International lawyers look to these authorities as evidence to determine whether a given norm can be deemed to have been accepted as a rule of international law. See The Paquete Habana, 175 U.S. 677 (1900); Restatement (Third), Reporters' Note 1 to § 102.

Article 38(1) is silent on the question whether the three sources it lists have the same hierarchic value, that is, whether treaties take precedence over custom and custom over general principles of law. Although there is some disagreement on the subject, in practice it would appear that an international court, faced with a dispute between two states, would give precedence to a specific treaty provision binding on the parties over a conflicting rule of customary international law, provided the latter did not have the status of a peremptory norm of international law (*jus cogens*) which a treaty may not nullify. Vienna Convention on the Law of Treaties, art. 53. See Chapter 5, § 5–13, infra. By the same token, a rule of customary international law would be given preference over a general principle of law. Thus there is a vague parallel between legislation, common law and legal principles in a domestic setting, on the one hand, and treaties, custom and general principles in an international context, on the other.

§ 2–3. **Customary international law.** Under article 38(1)(b) of the ICJ Statute "a general practice accepted as law" is an international custom. The Restatement (Third), § 102(2) provides a more meaningful and functionally sounder definition: "customary international law results from a general and consistent practice of states followed by them from a sense of legal obligation." Hence, a rule or principle, reflected in the practice or conduct of states, must be accepted by them, expressly or tacitly, as being legally binding on the international plane in order to be considered a rule of international law.

Customary international law develops from the practice of states. To international lawyers, "the practice of states" means official governmental conduct reflected in a variety of acts, including official statements at international conferences and in diplomatic exchanges, formal instructions to diplomatic agents, national court decisions, legislative measures or other actions taken by governments to deal with matters of international concern. Inaction can also be deemed a form of state practice.

A practice does not become a rule of customary international law merely because it is widely followed. It must, in addition, be deemed by states to be obligatory as a matter of law. This test will not be satisfied if the practice is followed out of courtesy or if states believe that they are legally free to depart from it at any time. The practice must comply with the *"opinio juris"* requirement, short for the Latin *opinio juris sive necessitatis*—a conviction that the rule is obligatory.

Although the *opinio juris* requirement may be implied from the fact that a rule has been generally and consistently followed over a long period of time, it is much more difficult to know how widely accepted a practice must be to meet the test. That it does not have to be universal seems to be clear. Equally undisputed is the conclusion that, in general, the practice must be one that is accepted by the world's major powers and by states directly affected by it. There must also not be a significant number of states that have consistently rejected it. Beyond that, it is difficult to be more specific. It should not be forgotten, however, that there exists a vast body of customary international law whose legal status is not disputed. Problems of proof arise primarily in areas of the law affected by ideological disputes or technological advances. See, e.g., North Sea Continental Shelf Cases (F.R.G. v. Denmark; F.R.G. v. Netherlands), 1969 ICJ 4.

Since international law is consensual in nature and since a practice does not have to be universally accepted to become a rule of customary international law, it follows that a state which has consistently rejected a practice before it became law, will not be bound by it. Although this is not a frequent occurrence, states may contract out of customary international law during its formative stage by refusing to consent to it. Cf. Fisheries Case (U.K. v. Norway), 1951 ICJ 116. But once a practice has acquired the status of law, it is obligatory for all states that have not objected to it.

There is some disagreement whether newly independent states are bound by all rules of international law in force at the time they become subjects of international law. The Restatement (Third), § 102, comment d., answers the question in the affirmative; this seems to be the better view. See Virally, "The Sources of International Law," in Manual of Public International Law 132, 137–39 (Sorensen ed. 1968).

§ 2–4. Conventional international law. In its enumeration of the sources of international law, article 38(1)(a) of the ICJ Statute speaks of "international conventions, whether general or particular, establishing rules expressly recognized by the contesting states." The reference here is to international agreements, both bilateral and multilateral. (For the law of treaties, see Chapter 5, infra.) Although a bilateral treaty between State A and State B would be a source of law in a dispute between them concerning an issue governed by the treaty, it is not a source of international law for the international community in general.

Some treaties can, however, give rise to or be a source of international law. The Restatement (Third) makes that point in § 102(3) in the following terms: "[i]nternational agreements create law for the states parties thereto and may lead to the creation of customary international law when such agreements are intended for adherence by states generally and are in fact widely accepted." These treaties can perform a function comparable to legislation on the domestic plane. Resort to this type of international law-making has increased dramatically in recent years, in part because customary international law usually develops much too slowly to meet the contemporary needs of the international community for new law.

In a formal sense, as the Restatement points out, these legislative or law-making treaties bind only the states parties to them. But to the extent that a very large number of states actually adheres to them or accepts their provisions as law, even without becoming parties to them, to that extent they can be viewed as an independent source of international law. Examples of such treaties are the Genocide Convention, the Vienna Convention on the Law of Treaties, the Vienna Convention on Diplomatic Relations, as well as various provisions of the UN Charter.

It is not always easy to distinguish these legislative treaties from agreements that are thought to be declaratory of preexisting customary international law. In one sense, the latter are merely evidence of what a group of states considers customary international law to be. The fewer the states that ratify the treaty or agree with the characterization, the less the weight that need be given to the evidence. On the other hand, if very many states adhere to the treaty or otherwise accept it as stating what the law is, the question whether it is declaratory of customary law loses significance. At some point, the agreement will come to be viewed as an independent source of general international law. The Vienna Convention on the Law of Treaties would appear to have gone through these law-making stages.

§ 2–5. **General principles of law.** Among the sources of international law listed in article 38(1) are "the general principles of law recognized by civilized nations." Today we speak of general principles of law recognized by or common to the world's major legal systems. Historically, general principles of law played an important role in the evolution of international law. The rules derived from them were often the only norms available and acceptable to states to regulate their international relations. They were accepted as a source of law on the theory that where states have universally applied similar principles in their domestic law, their consent to be bound by those same principles on the international plane could be inferred. The legal rules governing the responsibility of states for injuries to aliens were at one time based almost exclusively on that source.

Modern international law relies less and less on general principles of law as a source of law. This is so in part because many of the norms that were originally derived from general principles have over time become customary international law. The process of law-making by so-called legislative treaties has also reduced the need for general principles of law to fill substantive lacunae in the international legal system. That is why the Restatement (Third) quite soundly characterizes general principles as a "secondary source of international law." Id. § 102, Comment l.

General principles are still used to fill gaps, primarily for procedural matters and problems of international judicial administration. An international tribunal might resort to general principles, for example, to rule that the doctrine of *res judicata* or laches is part of international law, or that international judges have to conduct themselves in a manner that does not cast doubt on their impartiality or independence.

§ 2–6. **The character of modern international law.** The discussion in the preceding sections indicates that modern international law consists principally of conventional and customary international law. General principles perform an ever more marginal role as a source of law. The fact that legislative treaties now play an important role in the law-making process is beginning to transform international law into a more dynamic legal system. The development of customary international law is, on the whole, more cumbersome and consequently less suited for the fast pace of modern life.

III. SECONDARY SOURCES OR EVIDENCE

§ 2–7. Evidence of international law. Article 38(1)(d) lists judicial decisions and the views of duly qualified publicists "as subsidiary means for the determination of rules of law." This provision is generally understood to mean that the existence of a rule of international law may be proved by reference to the above mentioned "subsidiary means." Restatement (Third), § 103. They are cited by international lawyers as authoritative evidence that a given proposition is or is not international law.

Although the teachings of publicists and judicial decisions appear to be treated in article 38 as being of equal weight, this seems not to be true in practice. Not all judicial decisions, furthermore, have the same probative effect. Decisions of the International Court of Justice are by far the most authoritative on the international plane. For example, if the ICJ concludes that a given proposition has become a rule of customary international law, that holding, while not binding precedent in theory, is "the law" for all practical purposes. It would be extremely difficult, if not impossible, to refute such a holding on the international plane. Similarly, decisions of other modern international tribunals, particularly permanent ones, see Chapter 4, infra, are deemed to be highly authoritative. Much less importance attaches to decisions of domestic courts applying international law. What weight they will be given depends on the prestige and perceived impartiality of the national court, on whether the decision is in conflict with decisions of international courts, and on the forum where the decision is being cited. A decision of the U.S. Supreme Court interpreting international law is conclusive in the U.S., despite a contrary opinion even of the ICJ; but in Belgium, for example, the U.S. decision will most certainly be less authoritative than a decision of an international arbitral tribunal. The result would probably be the same in an American court, if it had to choose between a decision of the Belgian Supreme Court and that of an international tribunal.

The meaning of the phrase, "teachings of the most highly qualified publicists," must also be clarified. The reference here is not only to individual publicists or writers, although that is what was probably meant at one time. Today it includes entities such as the International Law Commission,

which was established by the UN to encourage
"the progressive development of international law
and its codification." UN Charter, art. 13(1)(a).
See also, Chapter 3, § 3–7, infra. The ILC is
composed of distinguished international lawyers
from all regions of the world. On the international plane, its conclusions would undoubtedly be considered more authoritative than the judicial opinions of domestic courts, for example. The
"teachings" of prestigious private scholarly institutions having a membership consisting of lawyers
from all major legal systems of the world would
also be accorded greater respect than some types of
judicial opinions. Note too that international lawyers trained in countries whose legal systems follow the Civil Law tradition are more likely to give
greater weight to scholarly writings than are Common Law lawyers, who tend to view judicial decisions in general as more authoritative. In an
American court, furthermore, the Restatement of
the Foreign Relations Law of the U.S., adopted by
the American Law Institute, would likely be given
greater weight as evidence of international law
than many types of foreign and international judicial opinions.

In recent decades, resolutions and similar acts of
intergovernmental international organizations
have acquired a very significant status both as
sources and as evidence of international law.
Some of these resolutions are legally binding on
the member states of the organizations. That is

true, for example, with regard to some UN Security Council resolutions, see UN Charter, arts. 24-25; Legal Consequences for States of the Continued Presence of South Africa in Namibia, Advisory Opinion, ICJ Reports 1971, p. 16, at 40-41. It is also true of various legislative measures promulgated by the International Civil Aviation Organization. See Buergenthal, Law-Making in the International Civil Aviation Organization 57 (1969). The binding character of these enactments is provided for in the treaties establishing the organizations. The resolutions in question consequently are a form of treaty law and, to that extent, a source of law.

The vast majority of resolutions of international organizations are not, however, formally binding in character. This is true, for example, of resolutions of the UN General Assembly. See Chapter 3, § 3-6 et seq., infra. Some of these resolutions (declarations, recommendations, etc.) can and do become authoritative evidence of international law. Restatement (Third), § 103, comment c. To understand how acts of international organizations acquire this status, it is important to recall that customary international law evolves through state practice to which states conform out of a sense of legal obligation. How states vote and what they say in international organizations is a form of state practice. Its significance in the law-making process depends upon the extent to which this state practice is consistent with the contemporaneous

conduct and pronouncements of states in other
contexts. Thus, for example, if a UN General
Assembly resolution declares a given principle to
be a rule of international law, that pronouncement
does not make it the law, but it is some evidence on
the subject. If the resolution is adopted unani-
mously or by an overwhelming majority, which
includes the major powers of the world, and if it is
repeated in subsequent resolutions over a period of
time, and relied upon by states in other contexts, it
may well reach the stage where its character as
being declaratory of international law becomes
conclusive. When that stage is reached is difficult
to determine, but that these resolutions play an
important part in the international law-making
process can no longer be doubted.

Of course, not very many measures adopted by
international organizations acquire this status.
The resolutions or declarations in question usually
have to proclaim one or more principles and identify them either as preexisting international law or
as rules that states in general should comply with
as a matter of law. These acts might be characterized as "legislative" resolutions that are not all
that dissimilar in their content or purpose from
the legislative treaties discussed in § 2–4, supra.
Resolutions dealing with human rights, decoloniza-
tion, outer space, ocean resources, environmental
issues, use of force, etc., are at times formulated to
perform that purpose. See, e.g., Case Concerning
Military and Paramilitary Activities in and against

Nicaragua (Nicaragua v. United States of America), Merits, ICJ 1986, p. 14, at 100–1 [hereinafter cited as Nicaragua v. U.S. (Merits)]; Advisory Opinion on Western Sahara, 1975 ICJ 612, at 23–33. It is not uncommon in some of these areas for the "legislative" declarations to be followed up by a formal treaty open to accession by the international community in general.

§ 2–8. **The law-making process.** Because of the consensual character of customary and conventional international law, and because of the absence of a centralized legislative or judicial system, states play a dual role in the law-making process: they act both as legislators and as advocates or lobbyists. See McDougal, "The Hydrogen Bomb Tests and the International Law of the Sea," 49 Am.J.Int'l L. 356–58 (1955). They are legislators or law-makers in the sense that the practice of states and the treaties which states conclude create international law. States also assert certain claims on the international plane in their diplomatic correspondence, in international courts, in international organizations, etc., through which they seek to obtain new rules of international law or to modify existing ones. Their individual assertions about what is or is not law, particularly customary law, is a form of lobbying or advocacy; it becomes law-making when these claims find the broad-based support that is required to transform them into law. Claims by governments about what

is or is not law must take the law-making consequences of their actions into account.

§ 2–9. Where to find the evidence. It is not
always easy to prove the existence of a practice
deemed by states to be obligatory, especially if
unambiguous judicial decisions or other authoritative pronouncements relating to it are not available. To gather the necessary proof, international
lawyers examine, *inter alia,* relevant government
pronouncements on the subject, national judicial
decisions, debates and resolutions of international
organizations, minutes and final acts of diplomatic
conferences. This search is frequently facilitated
by the availability of digests or compilations dealing with the international law practice of individual nations. A substantial number of countries
publish such works in various forms. Some are
excellent reference tools. For U.S. practice, the
most recent such work is Whiteman's multi-volume
Digest of International Law, supplemented by the
Annual Digest of United States Practice in International Law, both official publications of the U.S.
Department of State. A number of private collections containing decisions of national courts on
questions of international law are also available, as
are compilations of decisions of international arbitral tribunals and of permanent courts. International law treatises written by renowned legal
scholars in different parts of the world, some of
them available in various translations, are usually
also consulted and cited by international lawyers.

The UN and various regional organizations as well as individual countries publish official and unofficial collections of international agreements. See, e.g., the United Nations Treaty Series. Historical collections, especially those dealing with diplomacy, may also yield useful information concerning the existence of customary rules of international law. See, e.g., U.S. Department of State, U.S. Foreign Relations (multi-volume collection). For an overview of the reference material described in this section and for a guide to conducting international legal research, see Chapter 10, infra.

CHAPTER 3

INTERNATIONAL ORGANIZATIONS

I. INTRODUCTION

This chapter introduces the reader to the legal structure, function and role of so-called public or intergovernmental international organizations. See generally, Bowett, The Law of International Institutions (4th ed. 1982). These institutions should be distinguished from private or non-governmental international organizations (NGO's). The latter, of which there are many, include such well-known NGO's as Amnesty International, the International Law Association, and the International Committee of the Red Cross. These institutions are created under and governed by domestic, rather than international, law. Although they will not be dealt with in this chapter, it is worth keeping in mind that many of them play important roles in the promotion of international law and in its observance. See, e.g., UN Charter, art. 71.

Public or inter-governmental organizations are international institutions which are established by treaty and governed by international law. They have international legal personality to discharge the functions conferred on them and, to that extent, they are subjects of international law. Advisory Opinion on Reparation for Injuries Suffered in the Service of the United Nations, 1949 ICJ 3. They must have a permanent secretariat or institutional structure. Some authorities also assume that they must have a membership "consisting entirely or principally of states." Restatement (Third), § 217. The soundness of that assumption may be doubted. An international organization created exclusively by other organizations and not having states as members would qualify as an intergovernmental international organization. See Schermers, International Institutional Law 5–6 (1980).

Public international organizations have a relatively recent history. The earliest ones date from the second half of the 19th century, among them, the International Telegraphic Union (1865) and the Universal Postal Union (1874). The League of Nations, the International Labor Organization and a number of other smaller organizations were created after World War I. The United Nations and the majority of functional and regional international organizations in existence today came into being after World War II. The dramatic growth in the number of international organizations is the result of an ever-increasing recognition by governments of the international dimensions of the political, economic and social problems they face and of the need for international cooperation in resolving them. The powers, functions and structure of contemporary international organizations reflect the tension that exists between the reality of international interdependence and the reluctance of governments to relinquish some of their governmental authority to these organizations.

II. THE UNITED NATIONS

§ 3–1. **The UN Charter.** The United Nations came into being with the entry into force on October 24, 1945 of the UN Charter, which is a multilateral treaty that also serves as the constitution of the Organization. At the time of its founding, the UN had a membership of 51 states. Since then the number has more than tripled, and the UN now includes almost all the world's independent nations. Only Switzerland and Taiwan, the two Koreas, and a few mini-states are not members.

§ 3–2. **Nature and function.** The United Nations is a universal organization both in terms of its membership and the purposes it is designed to advance. It is an organization charged with peacekeeping responsibilities; with the development of friendly relations among nations; with the achievement of international cooperation in solving international problems of an economic, social, cultural and humanitarian character; with the promotion of human rights and fundamental freedoms for all human beings without discrimination. UN Charter, art. 1. In discharging these functions, the UN is enjoined from intervening in matters which are "essentially within the domestic jurisdiction" of any state. UN Charter, art. 2(7).

The meaning and significance of this prohibition has been extensively debated by legal scholars and diplomats. Article 2(7) has not, however, proved to be a serious obstacle to UN action despite the fact that it has been frequently invoked in UN debates. See, e.g., Higgins, The Development of International Law Through the Political Organs of the United Nations (1963).

§ 3-3. **International constitutional supremacy.** The UN Charter contains a supremacy clause which provides that "in the event of a conflict between the obligations of the Members of the United Nations under the present Charter and their obligations under any other international agreement, their obligations under the present Charter shall prevail." UN Charter, art. 103. This provision places the UN Charter at the apex in the hierarchy of international law norms, giving it a status on the international plane roughly comparable to that of a national constitution in domestic law.

§ 3-4. **The UN organs.** The principal organs of the UN are the General Assembly, the Security Council, the Economic and Social Council, the Trusteeship Council, the International Court of Justice, and the Secretariat. Some of these bodies have numerous subsidiary organs. The General Assembly is the only UN organ in which all member states have the right to be represented and to vote. The Assembly has plenary powers in the sense that it "may discuss any questions or any matters within the scope of the . . . Charter." UN Charter, art. 10. The Security Council has "primary responsibility for the maintenance of international peace and security." UN Charter, art. 24(1). It consists of 15 member states, five of them permanent members (China, France, USSR, United Kingdom, and the U.S.); the remaining members are elected to two-year terms in accordance with a formula that is designed to ensure an equitable geographic representation.

The Economic and Social Council (ECOSOC) consists of 54 member states elected by the General Assembly to three-year terms. To discharge its responsibilities in the economic, social and humanitarian areas, ECOSOC has established a large number of subsidiary organs with specialized competence in those fields. Among these are regional economic commissions and bodies, including the UN Commission on Human Rights and the UN Commission on the Status of Women. In the early days of the UN, the Trusteeship Council supervised the administration of many so-called non-self-governing territories. Today most of these territories are independent states and the Trusteeship Council has become an organ with greatly diminished responsibilities.

The Charter stipulates that the Secretariat "shall comprise a Secretary-General and such staff as the Organization may require." UN Charter, art. 97. The Secretary-General is elected to a five-year term by the General Assembly upon the rec-

ommendation of the Security Council. Since that
recommendation is subject to the veto power, the
Secretary-General can be elected only with the
acquiescence of the five permanent members of the
Security Council. Besides being the chief administrative officer of the Organization, the Secretary-
General has the power under article 99 of the
Charter to "bring to the attention of the Security
Council any matter which in his opinion may
threaten the maintenance of international peace
and security." This right of initiative is potential-
ly a very powerful political weapon, although it
has not been used to any significant extent.

The International Court of Justice is the princi-
pal judicial organ of the UN. UN Charter, art. 92.
Its functions are described in greater detail in
Chapter 4, infra.

§ 3–5. **Voting procedures.** Voting procedures
in the General Assembly differ from those in the
Security Council. Article 18 of the UN Charter,
which applies to the General Assembly, distinguishes between "important questions" and "other
questions." Resolutions involving "important
questions" require a two-thirds majority of the
members present and voting, while those dealing
with "other questions" require only a majority
vote. Besides expressly identifying some categories of questions as "important," the Charter provides that the Assembly may, by a majority vote,
determine additional categories of questions to

which the two-thirds majority rule shall apply. UN Charter, art. 18(3).

The rules governing voting in the Security Council distinguish between "procedural matters" and "all other matters." Resolutions on matters that are not "procedural" in character require nine affirmative votes, including "the concurring votes of the permanent members." UN Charter, art. 27(3). Under this rule, each of the five permanent members may veto the adoption of any resolution that is not "procedural." The Charter neither defines the meaning of "procedural matters" nor does it identify the categories of matters that are nonprocedural. Security Council practice indicates, however, that disagreements concerning whether a resolution is or is not subject to the veto power can be authoritatively resolved only by a vote which requires the concurring votes of the permanent members. This practice results in the so-called "double veto" procedure. It permits each permanent member to use its first veto to prevent the characterization of a resolution as "procedural" and the second veto to defeat the resolution itself. Abstentions by permanent members are not, however, deemed to constitute a veto. The mere absence of a permanent member will also not prevent the adoption of a Security Council resolution.

§ 3–6. Binding character of UN resolutions. The power of the General Assembly to adopt binding resolutions is extremely limited. Some of its decisions on budgetary matters are obligatory; so too are its instructions concerning the internal operations of the Organization. All other General Assembly resolutions are non-binding. They have the status of recommendations which the member states have no formal legal obligation to obey. UN Charter, arts. 10 and 14.

The powers of the Security Council are more extensive. It has the authority to adopt not only recommendations but also binding decisions. UN Charter, arts. 24–25; Advisory Opinion on the Legal Consequences for States of the Continued Presence of South Africa in Namibia (South West Africa) Notwithstanding Security Council Resolution 276 (1970), 1971 ICJ 17, at 52–53. Non-compliance with these decisions constitutes a violation of the Charter and may, in certain circumstances, result in the imposition of sanctions. UN Charter, arts. 41–42.

§ 3–7. **Law-making and legislative activities.** The subject matter jurisdiction of the Security Council and its power to adopt binding resolutions are, in principle, limited to matters which concern international peace and security. This means that the Security Council has no general law-making authority. The General Assembly, by contrast, has broad subject matter jurisdiction but lacks formal legislative authority because its resolutions do not have the force of law. The General Assembly does play a very important role, however, in the process by which international law is made and develops. See Chapter 2, § 2–7, supra.

Article 13(1)(a) of the UN Charter requires the General Assembly "to initiate studies and make recommendations . . . encouraging the progressive development of international law and its codification." The General Assembly has discharged this responsibility in various ways. In 1947, it established the International Law Commission. This body, composed of distinguished international lawyers, has drafted a number of important multilateral conventions that are now in force, including the Vienna Convention on the Law of Treaties and the Vienna Convention on Diplomatic Relations. Such major international human rights treaties as the UN Covenants on Human Rights and the UN Racial Convention were adopted and opened for signature by the General Assembly. Much of the existing international legislation relating to the law of the sea and to space law originated with the General Assembly or with diplomatic conferences that were convened by it. These codification efforts by the General Assembly have contributed significantly to the growth and modernization of international law.

Some resolutions of the General Assembly have also come to be accepted as declaratory of customary international law. The Universal Declaration of Human Rights, which was adopted by the General Assembly in the form of a resolution, is often cited as an example of a General Assembly resolution that has acquired this legal character. See generally Chapter 2, supra. Although the normative effect of UN resolutions is a highly controversial topic, few authorities dispute the fact that these resolutions have played and will continue to play an important role in the international lawmaking process. At the very least, widely supported and repeatedly reaffirmed UN resolutions reflect and articulate agreed upon principles on the basis of which international legal rules can and do develop. Hence, the statement that UN General Assembly resolutions are not binding, although true in a formal sense, contributes little to an understanding of the significant effect these resolutions at times have on the development of international law.

III. THE SPECIALIZED AGENCIES OF THE UNITED NATIONS

§ **3–8. Definition.** Despite their name, the so-called specialized agencies of the United Nations are neither organs nor subsidiary organs of the United Nations. They are autonomous international organizations having an institutional affiliation with the UN. That affiliation is provided for in article 57 of the UN Charter, which stipulates that "the various specialized agencies, established by intergovernmental agreement and having wide international responsibilities . . . in economic, social, cultural, educational, health, and related fields, shall be brought into relationship with the United Nations . . .."

§ 3–9. Organizations having specialized agency status. More than a dozen international organizations have obtained specialized agency status by concluding the necessary agreements with the UN. UN Charter, art. 63. Some of these organizations predate the UN itself, among them the International Telecommunications Union (ITU), the Universal Postal Union (UPU) and the International Labor Organization (ILO). Other well known specialized agencies are the United Nations Educational, Scientific and Cultural Organization (UNESCO), the International Civil Aviation Organization (ICAO), the World Health Organization (WHO), and the Food and Agriculture Organization (FAO). The two major international financial institutions—the World Bank and the International Monetary Fund (IMF)—also have specialized agency status.

§ 3–10. Member states. The membership roster of the specialized agencies is not necessarily identical to that of the UN. Not all UN member states belong to every specialized agency. This is particularly true of the IMF and the World Bank. On the other hand, all nations of the world are members of the UPU. Although a few organizations have cultivated a certain exclusivity, most specialized agencies strive for universal membership, but not all have achieved it.

§ **3–11. Legislative activities.** The specialized agencies are responsible for a large body of international legislation which greatly facilitates international commerce, transportation and communication. See generally, Kirgis, International Organizations in their Legal Setting 211 (1977). This is true, in particular, of the air navigation codes adopted by ICAO, the health regulations promulgated by WHO, the international standards established by the World Meteorological Organization (WMO), and the postal rules and regulations of the UPU. ILO has been responsible for a large number of treaties dealing with the protection of the rights and safety of workers around the world. These are but a few of the many examples that demonstrate the important legal contributions that the specialized agencies are making.

IV. REGIONAL ORGANIZATIONS

§ **3–12. General description.** Another important group of international institutions are regional and subregional intergovernmental organizations. They, too, are created by international agreements, which specify their functions and institutional structure. On the whole, the legal and institutional framework of these organizations resembles that of other intergovernmental international organizations. They differ from the latter principally in that their mandate is to deal with regional problems in general or with specific matters, be they economic, military or political in character.

§ 3-13. Basic characteristics. There exists a large number of regional and subregional institutions in all parts of the world. Their mandate, political significance and law-making powers vary substantially. A few enjoy extensive legislative or so-called supranational authority. This is true of the European Communities, which will be discussed in part V of this Chapter. Other regional and subregional organizations have the power to adopt only non-binding recommendations and/or draft treaties. The majority has some, albeit not very extensive, law-making authority. Some of them play a very important role in their regions, others are of only marginal significance, and a few exist on paper only. See generally, Encyclopedia of Public International Law, Instalment 4 (R. Bernhardt ed. 1981).

§ 3-14. Major regional organizations. Among the principal regional organizations are the Organization of African Unity (OAU), the Organization of American States (OAS), and the Council of Europe. The oldest of these is the OAS. Although it was established in its present form in 1948 with the entry into force of its Charter, the OAS traces its origins to the Union of American Republics which, together with its permanent secretariat—the Pan American Union—came into being during the first decade of the 20th century. Connell-Smith, The Inter-American System 37–76

(1966). The Council of Europe was created in 1949 and the OAU in 1963. In the sections that follow some of the functions and characteristics of these three organizations will be examined.

§ 3–15. **Membership requirements.** Unlike the OAS and the OAU, the Council of Europe restricts its membership to states committed to the rule of law and the enjoyment of human rights. Statute of the Council of Europe, art. 3. This requirement barred Spain and Portugal from becoming member states until they established democratic regimes; it also excludes the Soviet bloc countries. Today membership in the OAS is open to all independent American States. Until the entry into force in 1988 of the Protocol of Cartagena, which extensively revised the OAS Charter, states embroiled in territorial disputes with OAS member states were excluded from membership in the Organization pending the resolution of the disputes. This requirement has kept Guyana and Belize out of the OAS. OAU membership is open to any "independent sovereign African State." OAU Charter, art. IV. Countries ruled by white minority regimes are excluded, however.

§ 3–16. **Institutional structure.** The institutional structure of the Council of Europe differs from that of the two others in one important respect: it has an organ called the Parliamentary Assembly, consisting of elected representatives of the national parliaments of the member states. (In fact, the Council of Europe was the first intergovernmental organization to establish such an institution; it has since been created by a number of other regional and subregional organizations). Although the Assembly lacks genuine legislative power—it is principally a deliberative body—its existence opens the policymaking process of the Council of Europe to influence by individuals who are not government representatives.

§ 3–17. Functions and achievements.   The principal purpose of these three regional organizations is to promote cooperation between the states of their regions in a variety of different fields. OAS Charter, arts. 1–2; OAU Charter, art. II; Statute of the Council of Europe, art. 1.   In this regard, the OAU has put great emphasis on political cooperation, the Council of Europe has concentrated more on legal, social, and cultural issues, and the OAS has sought to make its influence felt both in political and other areas.   The Council of Europe has been particularly successful in drawing up and obtaining the ratification of a large number of treaties designed to facilitate commercial, cultural, scientific and educational interaction and cooperation within its region.   These are reproduced in the multi-volume treaty series of the Council of Europe, entitled "European Conventions and Agreements."   Although there exist a large number of inter-American treaties on similar subjects, the OAS has been less successful than the Council of Europe in obtaining their widespread acceptance and implementation.   See generally,

OAS Secretariat, The Inter-American System; Treaties, Conventions and Other Documents (vols. 1 and 2, 1983). Because the OAU is a much younger organization, many of whose members acquired their independence only in the past two decades (some of them after lengthy internal struggle), it has had little opportunity to develop much inter-African law. An institutional basis for such development does exist in the region, however. See generally, Sohn, 1 Basic Documents of African Regional Organizations (1971).

The OAS and the Council of Europe have each also established treaty-based regional human rights systems, which are supervised and enforced by judicial and quasi-judicial institutions. The OAU has adopted an African Charter on Human and Peoples' Rights, which entered into force in 1986. The Charter provides for the establishment of an African Commission on Human and Peoples' Rights, but it does not envisage the creation of a court. See Chapter 6, infra.

V.   SUPRANATIONAL ORGANIZATIONS

§ 3–18. Supranationality and the European Communities.   The concept of supranational organizations acquired practical significance with the entry into force in 1952 of the Treaty establishing the European Coal and Steel Community (ECSC), which uses that term. The ECSC was followed by the creation in 1958 of its two sister organizations—the European Economic Community (EEC) and the European Atomic Energy Community (Euratom). The three communities were subsequently merged for institutional purposes into the European Community, frequently also referred to as the European Common Market. Each Community does, however, retain some separate legal status because the substantive provisions of the three founding treaties continue, on the whole, to be applicable to each entity.

§ 3–19. The meaning of supranationality. Although international lawyers cannot agree on a definition of supranational organizations, the term is most often used to describe the European Communities. Schermers, supra, at 27–33; Hay, Federalism and Supranational Organizations (1966). (In fact, the European Communities are often considered to be the only existing supranational organization). What can be said in general about supranational organizations, using the European Communities as a point of reference, is that they have more governmental authority and law-making power in relation to their member states than do traditional international organizations. One key indicator of supranationality may well be the authority of the organization to make its law directly applicable to nationals of the member states without further execution by the national governments. As a practical matter, however, the only thing that can safely be said is that supranational organizations fall somewhere between federations and traditional international organizations in terms of the governmental powers they enjoy.

Kirgis, International Organizations in their Legal Setting 603 (1977).

§ 3–20. **Mandate of the European Communities.** The European Communities were established to bring about the economic integration of the national economies of the member states by doing away with all trade barriers *inter se* and by adopting a common economic policy, including customs duties, in relation to non-member states.   To achieve these objectives, the member states delegated to the Communities sweeping powers to regulate broad sectors of their economies, embracing the movement of goods, services, labor, transportation, etc.   Although what was once the ultimate goal of economic integration—political union—remains a distant dream, the Communities have in large measure succeeded in their efforts to forge an economic union or common market.

With the entry into force in 1987 of the Single European Act, the stage has been set for the full economic integration of the European Community. This treaty modifies and amplifies the Community treaties and fixes 1992 as the target date for the establishment of a so-called "internal market."   It requires the abolition of all frontiers between the member states and, to this end, provides for the free movement of goods, persons, services and capital by 1992.   See Single European Act, art. 13, reprinted in 25 Int'l Legal Mat. 506 (1986).   This treaty also contains provisions for greater European cooperation in the sphere of foreign policy, which is designed to advance the cause of European political integration.

Today the European Community consists of the following 12 member states: Belgium, Denmark, France, Germany, Greece, Ireland, Italy, the Netherlands, Luxembourg, Portugal, Spain and the United Kingdom.

§ 3–21. **The institutional structure of the Communities.** Four principal institutions are charged with the implementation of the policies of the Communities: the Council of Ministers, the Commission, the European Parliament, and the Court of Justice. Each member state has one representative on the Council. The Commission has 17 members, who are appointed by the member states acting in concert. In practice, each member state has the right to designate at least one commissioner; the remaining four seats are filled by nationals of the four largest countries (France, Germany, Italy and United Kingdom). Whereas the Council members are government representatives, the Commissioners are Community officials who serve in their personal capacities and as such are not permitted to receive instructions from their governments. The European Parliament consists of 518 representatives, elected in direct popular elections that are held in the member states. The Court of Justice consists of 13 judges who are designated by the member states acting in concert. See Chapter 4, infra, for a description of the role of the Court.

§ 3–22. Law-making in the Communities.

The Council is the principal repository of the legislative power of the Communities. The scope and extent of that power varies somewhat, however, depending upon the particular Community treaty that is being applied. The Commission shares some legislative power with the Council. Under the EEC Treaty, for example, the Council may as a rule only enact legislation that was proposed by the Commission, which also has some independent, albeit less significant, law-making authority. The European Parliament plays a minor role in the legislative process. Although the Council has an obligation to consult the Parliament, it is not required to follow the advice that is given. The Parliament does have the power, however, to force the resignation of the Commission as a whole. It also has the right to submit parliamentary questions about the policies and practices of the Communities and to approve the budget of the Communities. In 1987, the Single European Act, see § 3–20 supra, conferred additional functions on the European Parliament, although its legislative powers still fall far short of those that parliaments traditionally enjoy in democratic societies.

§ 3–23. Community law and domestic law.

Certain provisions of the Community treaties and various legislative measures of the Communities are directly applicable law within the member states, superseding domestic law in case of conflict. To that extent, the law of the Communities has a status within the member states comparable to

federal law in the United States. The Court of
Justice of the European Communities has repeatedly affirmed the supremacy of Community law
over national law and its direct applicability on the
domestic legal plane. See, e.g., Costa v. ENEL,
1964 Eur.Ct.Rep. 585. This conclusion is based on
two theories: the institutional theory, that the
member states transferred sovereignty to the Community in designated fields and thus gave up power to act inconsistently with Community norms, or
the political theory, that the member states have
agreed to limit their sovereignty in favor of the
Community, thus making any single unilateral act
ineffective if contrary to Community norms. See
Hay, supra, at 181.

The Court of Justice of the Communities super-
vises the uniform interpretation and application of
Community law. It does so in cases brought to it
by the Community institutions, the member states
and private enterprises, and in opinions rendered
at the request of domestic tribunals called upon to
apply Community law. The Community treaties
enable and, in certain instances, require these
courts to obtain an authoritative ruling from the
Court of Justice concerning Community law questions arising in cases being tried by them. See,
e.g., EEC Treaty, art. 177.

The pervasive impact of Community law on the
national legal systems of the member states, its
supremacy, and its direct and independent applicability on the domestic plane, distinguish that law

from the law of traditional international organizations. The legislative process of the Communities is also more independent of the will of the member states than is the legislative process of international organizations, which, as a rule, is under the exclusive control of governments. Viewed from this perspective, supranational organizations, as exemplified by the European Communities, represent a more advanced and more effective form of international cooperation than do traditional international organizations. See Stein, "Lawyers, Judges and the Making of a Transnational Constitution," 75 Am.J.Int'l L. 1 (1981).

VI. INTERNATIONAL ORGANIZATIONS, PEACE AND DEFENSE

§ 3–24. The UN and the use of force. The maintenance of international peace and security is a primary role of the United Nations under the Charter. Article 2(3) requires all members to "settle their international disputes by peaceful means in such a manner that international peace and security, and justice, are not endangered." Article 33(1) lists several peaceful dispute settlement mechanisms to serve as the first resort in lieu of force of arms. (These processes are discussed in Chapter 4, infra.) If settlement by these means fails, the parties must refer the dispute to the Security Council if the dispute poses a threat to the peace. UN Charter, art. 37(1). The Security Council "may . . . recommend appropriate procedures or methods of adjustment," including a call for further resort to peaceful measures. UN Charter, arts. 36(1) and 33(2). The International Court of Justice, in the *Namibia* case suggested that the Security Council's powers may exceed those specifically enumerated in the Charter to include any powers necessary to carry out its assigned peacekeeping task. See Advisory Opinion on Namibia, 1971 ICJ Rep. 16.

The General Assembly's formal role in peacekeeping is small, being restricted principally to its function as a forum for public discussion of the issues, UN Charter, arts. 10–12, 14, although the ICJ has suggested that the Assembly's role may be somewhat greater than the language of the Charter suggests. See Advisory Opinion on Certain Expenses of the United Nations, 1962 ICJ 151. Both the General Assembly and the Secretary General have the right to bring disputes that threaten the peace to the attention of the Security Council. UN Charter, arts. 11(3) and 99.

The principle that the use of force is prohibited in international relations is embodied in Article 2(4) of the UN Charter. It provides:

All Members shall refrain in their international relations from the threat or use of force against the territorial integrity or political independence of any state, or in any other manner inconsistent with the Purposes of the United Nations.

The full scope of this prohibition is not made clear by its language. Interpretations range from reading the paragraph as a total prohibition of the use of force (except in self-defense) to more limited interpretations that force is prohibited only when used to subjugate a nation or to take its territory or only when inconsistent with Charter purposes.

The use of force in self-defense has always been recognized as legitimate in international law. Article 51 of the Charter makes this explicit by permitting the use of force in self-defense "if an armed attack occurs" until the Security Council can take measures to restore peace. Whether such an armed attack must have actually occurred or only be imminent, thereby giving rise to a right of anticipatory self-defense, is still in dispute under the Charter. See generally, Nicaragua v. United States (Merits), 1986 ICJ Rep. 14.

Some authorities argue that the use of force is also permitted in furtherance of humanitarian objectives, for example, to protect one's own nationals abroad, to prevent human rights violations by a nation against its own citizens or to intervene in so-called wars of national liberation. Whether such action violates the terms of article 2(4) or is permitted on the ground that it is consistent with the purposes of the United Nations is a subject of continuing debate with the anti-interventionist forces having something the better of it.

§ 3–25. The UN and peacekeeping. The Security Council has primary responsibility for maintaining international peace and security. UN Charter, arts. 24 and 39. Under Chapter VII of the Charter, the Security Council has authority to invoke sanctions against nations engaged in a threat to the peace. UN Charter, arts. 39, 41 and 42. All member states are bound by such a decision. UN Charter, art. 25. The enforcement actions may be vetoed, however, by any of the five permanent members. The Security Council has been unable to obtain standing authority for the Permanent Military Force for peacekeeping envisioned in articles 43–47 of the Charter and must, therefore, together with the General Assembly, operate on an *ad hoc* basis in performing its peacekeeping role.

The Security Council has been able to authorize the collective use of force against armed attack only once, in Korea in 1950–53, while the Soviet Union was boycotting the Council and was therefore unable to cast a veto. When the USSR returned to the Security Council and blocked any further action, the General Assembly began to exercise some of the Council's power, relying to some extent on the so-called Uniting for Peace Resolution (1950), which provides in part as follows:

[The General Assembly] *Resolves* that if the Security Council, because of lack of unanimity of the permanent members, fails to exercise its primary responsibility for the maintenance of international peace and security in any case where there appears to be a threat to the peace, breach of the peace or act of aggression, the

General Assembly shall consider the matter immediately with a view to making appropriate recommendations to Members for collective measures, including in the case of a breach of the peace or act of aggression the use of armed force when necessary, to maintain or restore international peace and security.

On the whole, the United Nations has been ineffective in preventing large scale hostilities in which one or more of the world's major powers were involved directly or indirectly. In recent years, the UN has, however, had some success in dealing with hostilities in a number of cases through the use of a multilateral peacekeeping force.

Closely related to the political difficulties attendant upon any UN efforts to use military force to keep peace is the high cost of such operations. In the *Certain Expenses of the United Nations,* 1962 ICJ Rep. 151, the International Court of Justice found that expenses connected with the maintenance of peacekeeping forces in the Middle East and the Congo were properly expenses of the United Nations and could be assessed by the General Assembly. Despite this ruling, several countries refused to pay a share of these expenses.

§ 3–26. **Peacekeeping by regional organizations.** Articles 52–54 of the UN Charter permit the use of force by regional organizations to maintain international peace and security consistent with UN principles. The Security Council will encourage the peaceful settlement of local disputes by regional organizations but may direct enforcement actions through such organizations in specified situations. UN Charter, art. 53. But the use of force by these organizations is permitted only with Security Council authorization.

The here relevant regional organizations are found in the Americas, Africa, and the Middle East. In the inter-American system the fundamental agreements include the Inter-American Treaty of Reciprocal Assistance (the Rio Treaty) and the Charter of the Organization of American States. Both the Rio Treaty and the OAS Charter bind contracting parties not to use force against each other and authorize the collective use of force for defense or maintenance of peace and security on the continent. If an American state is attacked, the inherent right of self-defense under Article 51 of the United Nations Charter may be invoked. The regional agreements recognize the principle of collective self-defense to meet the attack. These treaties also recognize the territorial integrity and inviolability, sovereignty, and political independence of the parties. The charters of the Organization of African Unity (OAU) and the Arab League contain similar provisions.

§ 3–27. Regional defense treaties. Regional defense treaties should be distinguished from the regional organizations referred to in § 3–26, supra. The principal purpose of these arrangements is to provide for collective self-defense, a right explicitly recognized in article 51 of the UN Charter. Examples are the North Atlantic Treaty Organization (NATO), which includes many Western European states, the United States, and Canada. Its charter provides for collective self-defense, for peaceful settlement of disputes as well as for the promotion of development and cooperation. Another such arrangement is the Treaty of Friendship Cooperation and Mutual Assistance (Warsaw Pact), comprising the Soviet bloc nations of Eastern Europe, which obligates its members to mutual defense against outside attack. Yet another example is the Southeast Asia Treaty Organization (SEATO), which is based on the Southeast Asia Collective Defense Treaty of 1954. The treaty contained a separate Protocol that was applicable to Laos, Cambodia and Vietnam. The Protocol was relied upon as a legal basis for U.S. involvement in the Vietnam War.

CHAPTER 4

INTERNATIONAL DISPUTE SETTLEMENT

I. INTRODUCTION

This chapter deals with the traditional judicial, quasi-judicial and diplomatic institutions and methods that are used by the international community to resolve disputes between states. The procedures established under the UN Charter to prevent such disputes from leading to the use of force are treated in part VI of Chapter 3, supra. Here we describe the manner in which international law is applied to resolve international disagreements. See generally the two-part essay by Bilder, "An Overview of International Dispute Settlement," 1 Emory J.Int'l Disp.Res. 1 (1986) and id. at 131 (1987).

Article 33(1) of the UN Charter provides a useful list of the methods used to deal with international disputes. The article reads as follows:

The parties to any dispute, the continuance of which is likely to endanger the maintenance of international peace and security, shall, first of all, seek a solution by negotiation, enquiry, mediation, conciliation, arbitration, judicial settlement, resort to regional agencies or arrangements, or other peaceful means of their own choice.

In addition to reviewing the dispute settlement methods enumerated in article 33(1) of the UN Charter, this Chapter also describes the jurisdiction and functions of the permanent international courts in existence today. For a comprehensive overview, see Merrills, International Dispute Settlement (1984).

II. NON–JUDICIAL METHODS

§ 4–1. **Introduction.** The traditional non-judicial methods for the resolution of international disputes are negotiations, inquiry, mediation and conciliation. Depending upon the dispute, its context and the attitude of the parties to it, one or more and sometimes all of these methods may come into play. In short, they are not necessarily distinct or exclusive techniques for the resolution of a conflict. Each of these methods has domestic institutional counterparts which function in much the same way.

§ 4–2. **Negotiation.** Bilateral and multilateral negotiations to resolve differences between two or more states or between groups of states may be carried out by diplomatic correspondence, face-to-face encounters by permanent diplomatic envoys or by specially designated negotiators. Negotiation is the traditional and most commonly employed method. It tends to be the first stage in a process that may require resort to other, more formal, dispute-resolution methods. Prior negotiation is often also required as a condition precedent to the exercise of jurisdiction by an international court.

§ 4–3. **Inquiry.** The reference of a dispute to a process of inquiry involves the designation of a group of individuals or an institution to act as an impartial fact-finding or investigatory body. This method can be extremely effective under certain circumstances. An inquiry undertaken with the consent of the parties that results in an unambiguous finding of fact is more likely than not to lead to the resolution of the dispute when the disagreement between the parties involves only issues of fact.

§ 4–4. **Mediation or good offices.** This technique consists of third-party efforts to assist the parties to a dispute to resolve their disagreements through negotiation. The role of mediator is to bring the parties together, to serve as intermediary between them, to propose solutions and to explore opportunities for settlement. Today these techniques take on many different forms. Mediators may serve as a bridge between contending states whose representatives do not even talk to each other—the Middle East shuttle diplomacy provides a good example. Mediators may sit in on negotiations, chair meetings, suggest solutions, cajole, etc.

§ 4–5. **Conciliation.** This is a more formal process than the other dispute resolution techniques described above. It requires an agreement by the parties to the dispute to refer the controversy to a group of individuals or to an institution to make appropriate findings of fact and recommendations. As a rule, the parties do not obligate themselves to accept the recommendations, but the existence of a report containing the findings tends to make it more difficult for the parties to disregard it or to reject the recommendations, particularly if they wish to avoid the appearance of acting in an arbitrary or lawless manner.

§ 4–6. **Negotiation, mediation, conciliation combined.** There exist today numerous international institutions and mechanisms in which the above mentioned techniques are structured into one formal dispute-resolution process that consists of a combination of negotiation, fact-finding, mediation and conciliation. Institutions that have been established to resolve disputes concerning claims of human rights violations are but one example of this phenomenon. They normally consist of a committee or commission created by a treaty, which as a rule also contains a catalog of the protected rights. Disputes concerning violations of these rights may be referred by the states parties to a committee. That body then initiates a formal process which moves from negotiations and fact-finding to efforts to bring about a friendly settlement, followed by a report containing conclusions and, if a friendly settlement is not reached, recommendations. See, e.g., UN Racial Convention, arts. 11–13; International Covenant on Civil and Political Rights, arts. 41–42. In some of these treaties, provisions are even made for adjudication, which is

resorted to as a final step in the dispute-settlement
process. This possibility exists, for example, under
the European and American Conventions of
Human Rights. For an overview, see Buergenthal,
International Human Rights in a Nutshell (1988).
A much more complex machinery for the resolution of disputes, which draws on all the aforementioned techniques in a variety of different contexts
and combinations, has been established by the Law
of the Sea Treaty. See Sohn & Gustafson, The
Law of the Sea in a Nutshell, ch. XII (1984). The
UN Charter itself envisages a dispute resolution
process in which the Security Council and the
General Assembly play different roles in activating
resort to the various methods listed in Article 33 of
the Charter. UN Charter, chs. VI & VII.

III. QUASI–JUDICIAL METHODS

§ 4–7. **Arbitration and adjudication distinguished.** International arbitration and international adjudication differ from the dispute-resolution techniques discussed in the preceding sections
in one very important respect: both the arbitral
and judicial decisions are binding on the parties.
In international law, arbitration is a form of adjudication, the difference being that an arbitral tribunal or panel is as a rule not a permanent judicial body. Its composition, as well as its
jurisdiction and the rules of procedure it applies,
must be agreed upon by the parties. (The agreement in which all of these matters are settled is

known as a *compromis.*) International adjudication, by contrast, takes place in the context of a permanent court, which has a fixed composition and operates under preexisting jurisdictional standards and rules of procedure.

§ 4–8. **International arbitral clauses.** In practice, at least three types of international arbitral agreements can be identified. The first consists of an arbitration clause that is included in a treaty, be it bilateral or multilateral, that deals with one or more other substantive matters. The function of this clause is to provide a method for the resolution of disputes that might arise in the interpretation or application of that particular treaty. It is not uncommon to find such a clause in bilateral commercial treaties (so-called treaties of friendship, commerce and navigation or FCN treaties, for example) or in international civil aviation agreements.

The second type of arbitral agreement consists of treaties whose sole function is to establish a method for the resolution and arbitration of whatever disputes or categories of disputes might arise between the parties in the future. The best known agreements of this type are the 1899 Hague Convention for the Pacific Settlement of International Disputes, as revised by the 1907 Hague Convention, and the 1928 General Act for the Pacific Settlement of International Disputes, which was amended in 1949. The Hague Conventions established the Permanent Court of Arbitration which,

despite its name, is not a court but an institution
for the facilitation of international arbitration. It
maintains a roster of arbitrators, drawn from lists
of four individuals presented by each of the states
parties as being qualified to serve on arbitral
panels or tribunals. These bodies have been and
continue to be used by states to decide disputes.

In the third category are arbitral agreements
that are concluded to deal with an existing dispute
which the parties have not been able to settle by
other means. A recent example is the agreement
between the U.S. and Iran to arbitrate their outstanding claims, which has led to the establishment of the Iran-U.S. Claims Tribunal. See Declaration Concerning the Settlement of Claims by the
Government of the United States of America and
the Government of the Islamic Republic of Iran of
January 19, 1981, 10 Int'l Leg.Mat. 230 (1981).

§ 4–9. Consent to arbitrate. It is a basic rule
of international law that states cannot be required
to arbitrate a dispute unless they have given their
consent thereto, either before or after the controversy has arisen. The first two types of arbitral
agreements mentioned in § 4–8, supra, often contain provisions permitting either party to the dispute to require the other party to arbitrate. But
where this is not true, the subsequent consent of
both parties will be needed for arbitration to take
place. In the third type, the consent to arbitrate is
contained in the *compromis*.

§ **4-10. The *compromis*.** This agreement contains provisions for the designation of the arbitral panel, if that subject has not been previously agreed upon. It will identify the issues that are to be decided, specify the rules of procedure to be followed, and state the undertaking of the parties to abide by and implement the award. Since the *compromis* is a binding international agreement, a party's failure to abide by the award would constitute a separate breach of international law. The vast majority of international arbitral awards are complied with.

§ **4-11. Composition of arbitral tribunals.** Usually, arbitral tribunals are composed of three members. Each party to the dispute may name one member, with the third member to be designated by agreement of the parties or, failing such agreement, by the President of the International Court of Justice or some other person of international stature. If the parties are unable to agree on the third member and the arbitral agreement does not contain an alternative method for his selection, there may be no way to implement the agreement to arbitrate because international courts have no general power under international law to impose an arbitrator. While arbitral tribunals vary in size—the U.S.-Iranian Claims Tribunal, for example, consists of nine members—the tripartite structure described above is usually maintained. Arbitral tribunals are established either to deal with a specific dispute or to decide a variety of claims. In some instances, so-called *ad*

hoc international arbitral tribunals have continued
to function for decades.

§ 4–12. **The arbitral award.** Unless the
agreement provides otherwise, arbitral awards are
binding on the parties to the dispute and not
subject to appeal. Some arbitral clauses permit
judicial review of the decree by the International
Court of Justice. See, e.g., Appeal Relating to the
Jurisdiction of the ICAO Council (India v. Paki-
stan), 1972 ICJ Rep. 46. The validity of arbital
awards may be challenged, moreover, in certain
special circumstances. The four most commonly
accepted bases for such a challenge, codified in the
UN's Model Rules of Arbitral Procedure, are that
the tribunal has exceeded its powers; that there
was corruption on the part of a member of the
tribunal; that there has been failure to state the
reasons for the award or a serious departure from
a fundamental rule of procedure; that the undertaking to arbitrate or the *compromis* is a nullity.
UN Model Rules on Arbitral Procedure, art. 35.
These rules were approved by the UN General
Assembly in 1958. See generally, Restatement
(Third) § 904.

§ 4–13. **Applicable law and sources of law.**
Arbitral tribunals apply international law unless
the parties specify that some other law should be
applied. In the 19th and early 20th centuries and
before, international law case law consisted principally of decisions of arbitral tribunals and judgments of domestic courts applying international

law. (The Central American Court of Justice rendered only a handful of decisions during its brief existence between 1908 and 1918, and the Permanent Court of International Justice was not established until 1920. See part IV, infra.)

Although the authority of the older arbitral decisions has diminished with time and some have been characterized by new states as relics of colonialism and imperialism, they remain a valuable secondary source of law. The legal authority of contemporary arbitral decisions is much greater, of course. In the absence of a decision by the International Court of Justice or one of the other permanent courts, these decisions are the best judicial evidence of international law.

§ 4–14. **International arbitration and the individual.** Although international arbitration is a method for the adjudication on the international plane of disputes between states, the facts giving rise to such disputes often involve claims by nationals of one state against another state. Here the states are said to be "espousing" the claims of their nationals. Over the years, international arbitral tribunals have developed a whole body of international law, both procedural and substantive, bearing on the various legal issues that arise in the litigation of such claims. See Chapter 6, infra. Much of that law, particularly its procedural and jurisdictional components, has found its way into the constitutions and rules of procedures of existing international courts.

IV. INTERNATIONAL COURTS

§ 4–15. Introduction. International courts, that is, permanent international judicial institutions, are a relatively recent phenomenon of international life. The Central American Court of Justice (1908–1918) was the first such tribunal. It did not survive the periodic upheavals dividing the five Central American republics (Costa Rica, Honduras, Guatemala, Nicaragua, and El Salvador) which established it. This tribunal holds a special place in the history of international courts, not only because it was the first, but also because under its charter individuals had standing to institute proceedings against governments. The recognition of such a right remains a revolutionary concept in international adjudication. Today there exist a number of permanent international courts, including the International Court of Justice (ICJ) and various specialized regional tribunals, which will be discussed in the remainder of this chapter.

One very important rule applicable to international adjudication needs to be emphasized at this point: under international law, states cannot be required to submit disputes to international adjudication unless they have consented to it. Thus, the threshold question for an international tribunal hearing a case always is the issue whether its jurisdiction has been accepted by the states parties to the dispute. States are free, as a rule, to accept jurisdiction either before a dispute has arisen or thereafter, to limit their acceptance to certain types of disputes, and to attach various conditions to the acceptance. Jurisdictional issues consequently always loom large in the work of international tribunals.

A. The International Court of Justice

§ 4–16. **Historical development.** The ICJ is the successor to the Permanent Court of International Justice (PCIJ), which was established in 1920 under the auspices of the League of Nations. The PCIJ stopped functioning during the Second World War in 1939, although it was not formally dissolved until 1946. That tribunal rendered some 30 judgments, 27 advisory opinions, and various interlocutory orders. These decisions continue to be cited as authority by international lawyers and judges.

The ICJ, which is the principal judicial organ of the UN, came into being in 1945. Its Statute or constitution, modelled on that of the PCIJ, is annexed to and forms an integral part of the UN Charter. All member states of the UN are *ipso facto* parties to the Statute of the Court. States that are not UN members may adhere to the Statute under conditions that the UN has prescribed. UN Charter, arts. 92–94.

§ 4–17. **Composition and institutional structure.** The ICJ consists of 15 judges, no two of whom may be nationals of the same state. The judges are elected by the UN General Assembly and the Security Council; they have to receive an absolute majority of the votes in both bodies. The regular term of the judges is nine years; they may be reelected. There is no formal rule allocating a seat on the Court to each of the permanent members of the Security Council, although this is done in practice.

The Court has two distinct types of jurisdiction: contentious jurisdiction and advisory jurisdiction. Different rules and procedures apply to each.

1. Contentious Jurisdiction

§ 4–18. **Bases of contentious jurisdiction.** The contentious jurisdiction of the ICJ applies only to disputes between states which have accepted that jurisdiction. The Court lacks contentious jurisdiction to deal with disputes involving individuals or entities that are not states. ICJ Statute, art. 34(1).

In discussing the Court's jurisdiction, it is important not to confuse adherence to the Court's Statute with jurisdiction. The doors of the Court are open to a state which is a party to its Statute—that is what adherence to the Statute signifies. But whether the Court may hear a case filed by a state party to the Statute against another state party depends upon whether both have accepted the tribunal's jurisdiction.

Article 36 of the Statute deals with the Court's contentious jurisdiction. There are basically three ways in which states can submit to the jurisdiction of the ICJ. First, they can accept the Court's jurisdiction on an *ad hoc* basis for the adjudication of an existing dispute. ICJ Statute, art. 36(1). Second, they can adhere to a treaty, be it bilateral or multilateral, in which the Court's jurisdiction is accepted, expressly or by implication, for cases relating to the interpretation or application of the treaty or for any other disputes that might arise. Ibid. Provisions of this type may be limited to specific disputes or be general in character. Third, under article 36(2), which is known as the "optional clause," the states parties to the Statute may by means of a unilateral declaration undertake that "they recognize as compulsory *ipso facto* and without special agreement, in relation to any other state accepting the same obligation, the jurisdiction of the Court in all legal disputes . . ." involving issues of law or fact governed by rules of international law. The Court lacks jurisdiction to hear cases that are governed by domestic law rather than international law. ICJ Statute, art. 38(1).

§ 4–19. **Reciprocity.** A state's unilateral declaration accepting the Court's jurisdiction under article 36(2) is applicable "in relation to any other state accepting the same obligation." By filing this declaration, a state accepts the Court's jurisdiction on the basis of reciprocity and, consequently, is required to respond only if sued by a state that has made a similar declaration.

Moreover, whatever jurisdictional defenses the appellant state might have been able to assert against the respondent under its declaration if the roles were reversed, are open to the respondent because of reciprocity. As the ICJ has explained in the leading case on the subject, "since two unilateral declarations are involved, such jurisdiction is conferred upon the Court only to the extent to which the two Declarations [of france and norway] coincide in conferring it." Case of Certain Norwegian Loans (France v. Norway), 1957 ICJ 9, at 23–24. But see Nicaragua v. U.S. (Jurisdiction), 1984 ICJ Rep. 392, 417–19.

The reciprocity principle has special significance because a majority of the forty-odd states which have accepted the Court's jurisdiction under article 36(2) have done so with various reservations. The Court's jurisdiction is consequently narrowed in any case in which one of the parties to the dispute has a reservation, because the party that has not made the reservation may nevertheless invoke it against the other party. Interhandel Case (Switzerland v. United States), 1959 ICJ 6, at 23. For example, in the *Norwegian Loans* case, supra, France, which filed the action against Norway, had accepted the Court's jurisdiction under article 36(2) with a reservation providing that "this declaration does not apply to differences relating to matters which are essentially within the national jurisdiction as understood by the government of the French Republic." The Norwegian declaration contained no reservation. Under the principle of reciprocity, which was expressly reiterated in the

Norwegian declaration, Norway was permitted to "except from the compulsory jurisdiction of the Court disputes understood by Norway to be essentially within its national jurisdiction." Ibid. Most commentators agree that the result would have been the same, even if the Norwegian declaration had merely repeated the text of article 36(2) without reiterating that its acceptance was "on condition of reciprocity."

The question whether a state, which accepts the Court's jurisdiction "unconditionally," will be deemed to have waived reciprocity under article 36(2), has been answered in the negative by a majority of commentators. They suggest that the stipulation in article 36(3) of the Statute that article 36(2) declarations "may be made unconditionally or on condition of reciprocity on the part of several or certain states, or for a certain time," was not designed to affect the principle of reciprocity proclaimed in article 36(2). Instead, it was inserted to enable states to condition the entry into force of their declaration upon the acceptance of the Court's jurisdiction by certain other states. It would appear, therefore, that a state which has accepted the Court's jurisdiction under article 36(2) and declared it to be "unconditional" would be entitled to invoke the reservation of any state that filed an action against it. Cf. Nicaragua v. U.S. (Jurisdiction), supra.

§ 4–20. **The Connally reservation.** The United States accepted the Court's jurisdiction under article 36(2) in 1946. It did so with a number of reservations, however. Most important was the so-called "Connally Amendment," named for the Texas Senator who proposed it. The reservation excluded from the jurisdiction of the Court "disputes with regard to matters which are essentially within the domestic jurisdiction of the United States of America as determined by the United States of America." The purpose of this reservation or so-called "self-judging" clause was to ensure that the U.S. and not the ICJ would decide, as a practical matter, whether a dispute is "domestic" in character and consequently outside the Court's jurisdiction. Given the principle of reciprocity, this reservation had the effect of entitling any state the U.S. might wish to sue to invoke the reservation against the U.S., which would require the Court to dismiss the suit. See Gross, "Bulgaria Invokes the Connally Amendment," 56 Am.J.Int'l L. 357 (1962).

It has been argued from time to time that the Connally Amendment and similar self-judging clauses are invalid because they violate article 36(6) of the Statute of the Court, which provides that "in the event of a dispute as to whether the Court has jurisdiction, the matter shall be settled by the decision of the Court." The ICJ has not addressed this issue, although it had the opportunity to do so in a number of cases. Judge H. Lauterpacht, an eminent international lawyer, considered the question in the *Norwegian Loans* case, supra, at 101–02, and in the *Interhandel* case, supra, at

95, and concluded that such self-judging clauses violate the Statute. A similar view was expressed by Judge Schwebel in his dissenting opinion in *Nicaragua v. U.S.* (Jurisdiction), supra, at 601–02.

The debate over the wisdom of the Connally reservation became academic when the U.S. gave notice in 1985 of its decision to terminate U.S. acceptance of the jurisdiction of the ICJ under Article 36(2) of its Statute. This termination became effective in 1986 and was prompted by the U.S. Government's dissatisfaction with the U.S.– Nicaragua litigation. See § 4–21, infra; "United States: Department of State Letter and Statement concerning Termination of Acceptance of I.C.J. Compulsory Jurisdiction," 24 Int'l Leg.Mat. 1742 (1985).

The withdrawal by the U.S. of its acceptance of the Court's jurisdiction under Article 36(2) does not affect the Court's jurisdiction over the U.S. under Article 36(1). The U.S. is a party to many treaties that confer jurisdiction on the Court under that provision of its Statute, enabling the U.S. to sue and be sued thereunder.

§ 4–21. The "Nicaragua" amendment. In its 1946 acceptance of the Court's jurisdiction under article 36(2), the U.S. had also provided "that this declaration shall remain in force for a period of five years and thereafter until the expiration of six months after notice may be given to terminate this declaration." This declaration remained in force in its 1946 form until 1984, when the U.S. sought to amend it as follows:

> The aforesaid [1946] declarations shall not apply to disputes with any Central American state arising out of or related to events in Central America, any of which disputes shall be settled in such a manner as the parties to them may agree.

> Notwithstanding the terms of the aforesaid declaration, this proviso shall take effect immediately and shall remain in force for two years . . ..

This amendment was prompted by Nicaragua's decision to file suit against the U.S. in the ICJ. Having learned of Nicaragua's intention a few days before the action was instituted, the U.S. sought to block it with the amendment. The ICJ upheld Nicaragua's contention that the U.S. was bound by the six-months notice requirement contained in the 1946 declaration, despite the fact that Nicaragua's reservation contained no notice provision and could have been withdrawn at any time. Justifying its refusal to permit the U.S. to rely on the principle of reciprocity, the Court ruled that "reciprocity cannot be invoked in order to excuse departure from the terms of a state's own declaration, whatever its scope, limitation or conditions." Nicaragua v. United States (Jurisdiction), supra, at 419.

§ 4–22. **National security considerations.** Issues of national security are usually perceived to be the most sensitive and, thus, least likely to be submitted to international adjudication. For example, in recent decades several nations have modified their acceptance of the compulsory jurisdiction of the ICJ to exclude matters related to national security or self-defense. The U.S., which had not made such a modification, cited these considerations, *inter alia*, as reasons for its withdrawal from the *Nicaragua* case after the Court ruled against it on the jurisdictional issue. See U.S. Statement of January 8, 1985, 24 Int'l Leg. Mat. 246 (1985). Similar considerations explain the French position in the *Nuclear Test Cases (Austria v. France; New Zealand v. France)*, 1973 ICJ 99 and 135; 1974 ICJ 253 and 257. In the *Nicaragua* case, the ICJ rejected the view that disputes involving issues of national security or self-defense were *ipso facto* not suitable for adjudication by the Court or inadmissible. Nicaragua v. United States (Jurisdiction), supra, at 433–37. The Court amplified on this view in its subsequent judgment in the *Nicaragua* case, which it decided against the United States on the merits. Nicaragua v. U.S. (Merits), 1986 ICJ Rep. 14. For different assessments of this case, see "Appraisal of the ICJ's Decision: Nicaragua v. United States (Merits)," 81 Am J. Int'l L. 77 (1987).

§ 4–23. **Effect and enforcement of judgments.** Judgments rendered by the ICJ in contentious cases are binding on the parties thereto. ICJ Statute, art. 59. They are also deemed to be "final and without appeal." ICJ Statute, art. 60. The

Statute of the Court does not specify how its judgments are to be enforced. That subject is governed by article 94 of the UN Charter. In article 94(1), each UN member state "undertakes to comply with the decision of the International Court of Justice in any case to which it is a party." A state which fails to abide by the Court's judgment would thus violate the UN Charter. This point is reinforced by article 94(2), which permits a party to a suit to appeal non-compliance to the UN Security Council, "which may, if it deems necessary, make recommendations or decide upon measures to be taken to give effect to the judgment." It should be emphasized that the Security Council "may" but need not take any action. Moreover, if it acts, it may do so by means of a recommendation or decision; only the latter is binding. The failure of a member state to comply with a Security Council decision may in certain circumstances give rise to enforcement measures. See UN Charter, arts. 39, 41, 42. Since the veto power of the permanent members applies to enforcement measures, that action will only be taken in cases in which these states are prepared to cooperate in forcing compliance with a judgment of the Court. The same is true of their willingness to support the original resolution. For a U.S. veto of a Security Council resolution on the subject, see 25 Int'l Leg.Mat. 1337, at 1352–65 (1986).

2. *Advisory Jurisdiction*

§ 4–24. Scope of advisory jurisdiction. The advisory jurisdiction of the ICJ may be invoked only by UN organs and by the specialized agencies of the UN. ICJ Statute, art. 65(1). States and individuals have no standing to request advisory opinions. Article 96(1) of the UN Charter expressly authorizes the UN General Assembly and the Security Council to seek advisory opinions. Other UN organs and the specialized agencies of the UN may do so with the approval of the General Assembly. UN Charter, art. 96(2). The Assembly has given this authorization not only to the principal organs listed in article 7 of the UN Charter, but also to various subsidiary organs. As for the authority of the specialized agencies to request advisory opinions, the requisite approval is, as a rule, contained in their cooperative agreements with the UN. See Keith, The Extent of the Advisory Jurisdiction of the International Court of Justice 36–41 (1971).

§ 4–25. Legal character. Advisory opinions are by definition non-binding. Whether the requesting institution will be guided by or accept as obligatory the Court's ruling is a matter that is governed by the institution's internal law. In the UN it is customary for the requesting organ to vote on whether to accept the opinion. Some international agreements provide that the advisory opinion requested by an organization is binding on the organization and the states parties. See Pomerance, The Advisory Function of the International Court in the League and UN Eras 388–90 (1973). The non-binding character of advisory opinions should not be confused with their juridical authority, the legitimating effect they may have on the conduct of states and organizations, or with their value as precedent in a legal system in which there is a scarcity of judicial pronouncements. In practice, advisory opinions are relied upon and cited as legal authority as frequently as are judgments rendered in contentious cases. Since the doctrine of *stare decisis* (binding precedent) is not a doctrine of international law and since it does not apply to contentious decisions of the ICJ, the Court's advisory opinions have in theory no less precedential value than judgments rendered in contentious cases. The fact that the latter are binding on the parties to the case and that the former are not does not affect their value as legal precedent in future controversies involving other parties.

B. Other International Courts

§ 4–26. **Introduction.** In addition to the ICJ, which is the only permanent international court of a universal character, there exist a number of permanent regional international courts with highly specialized jurisdiction. Among the most active of these, three sit in Western Europe and one in the Americas.

§ 4–27. **Court of Justice of the European Communities.** The busiest international tribunal is the 13-judge Court of Justice of the European

Communities. This Court, which renders roughly
150 judgments annually, is the judicial organ of
the European Common Market. See Chapter 3,
supra. The Court has its seat in Luxembourg and
was established in 1952 with the creation of the
European Coal and Steel Community. Its jurisdiction was expanded in 1958 when the European
Economic Community and the European Atomic
Energy Community were created. The separate
Community treaties confer similar, but not identical, powers on the Court of Justice.

The Court's principal function is the interpretation and application of the constitutive instruments of the Communities and of the legislative
measures emanating from the bodies established
by them. See Bebr, Development of Judicial Control of the European Communities (1981). The
jurisdiction of the Court extends to disputes involving the member states and the authorities of the
Communities. Private enterprises and individuals
may also refer certain types of cases to the Court.
Moreover, the national courts of the member states
may, and in some circumstances must, request the
Court to provide them with rulings interpreting
questions of Community law arising in domestic
litigation. The authority to render these rulings
was conferred on the Court to ensure the uniform
interpretation of Community law by the courts of
all member states. In this sense it roughly paral-
lels the federal question jurisdiction of the U.S.
Supreme Court. See Stein, "Lawyers, Judges and

the Making of a Transnational Constitution," 75 Am.J.Int'l L. 1 (1981).

§ 4–28. **European Court of Human Rights.** Another busy regional tribunal is the European Court of Human Rights, established in 1959. It is the judicial organ of the European Convention of Human Rights. That treaty was concluded within the institutional framework of the Council of Europe, the 21-member Western European regional intergovernmental organization which is located in Strasbourg, France. See Chapter 3, supra. The jurisdiction of the Court extends to the interpretation and application of the European Convention and its various Additional Protocols. See generally, Buergenthal, International Human Rights in a Nutshell 106 (1988).

Only the states parties to the Convention and the European Commission of Human Rights may refer cases to the Court, provided the states parties concerned have accepted the tribunal's jurisdiction. Individuals do not have the right to take cases to the Court. They may only file complaints with the Commission. From there the case may go to the Court if the Commission or an interested state decides that it should be taken to the tribunal. In recent years, individual litigants and their counsel have gained the right to be heard by the Court in their cases. Although few cases were referred to the European Court in the first decade of its existence, it now receives some 30 to 40 annually. Its growing case law is beginning to have a significant impact on the protection of civil liberties in the states parties, making the Court, for all practical purposes, the highest constitutional tribunal of Western Europe. See Higgins, "The European Convention on Human Rights," in Human Rights in International Law: Legal and Policy Issues 495 (Meron ed. 1984). See also, Merrills, The Development of International Law by the European Court of Human Rights (1988).

§ 4–29. **Benelux Court of Justice.** This tribunal was established in 1974 by Belgium, the Netherlands and Luxembourg. It has its permanent seat in Brussels, Belgium. Although the Court is not, as such, an institution of the Benelux Economic Union, its function is to ensure uniformity in the interpretation of the large number of Benelux treaties concluded by the states parties to advance the objectives of the Union. Thus, with each new Benelux treaty, the Court acquires additional jurisdiction. The specific powers of the Court resemble those of the Court of Justice of the European Communities on which it was modelled. See Kruijtbosch, "Benelux Economic Union, College of Arbitrators and Court Justice," Encyclopedia of Public International Law, Instalment No. 6, at 39 (1983).

§ 4–30. **Inter-American Court of Human Rights.** The seven-judge Inter-American Court of Human Rights was established in 1979. It has its seat in San Jose, Costa Rica. The Court is the judicial organ of the American Convention on

Human Rights, which entered into force in 1978. This treaty is modelled on the European Convention of Human Rights and envisages a similar institutional structure, consisting of the Court and the Inter-American Commission on Human Rights. But unlike its European counterpart, the Inter-American Court has extensive powers to render advisory opinions interpreting the Convention as well as other human rights treaties. The contentious jurisdiction of the Inter-American Court resembles that of the European Court. Only the Commission and the member states that have accepted the Court's jurisdiction have standing to bring cases to it; individuals lack the right to do so. Complaints filed with the Commission by private individuals may be referred to the Court by the Commission or an interested member state. See Buergenthal, "The Inter-American Court of Human Rights," 76 Am.J.Int'l L. 231 (1982); Buergenthal, "The Advisory Practice of the Inter-American Court of Human Rights," 79 Am.J.Int'l L. 1 (1985). The Court has to date decided more advisory opinions than contentious cases.

CHAPTER 5

THE INTERNATIONAL LAW OF TREATIES

I. INTRODUCTION

Treaties perform a variety of functions on the international plane that in domestic law are performed by many different types of legal acts and instruments, including constitutions, laws of general applicability, contracts, deeds, trust agreements, corporate charters, etc. Treaties, by contrast, serve as the constitutions of international organizations, see Chapter 3, supra, they can be a source of general international law, see Chapter 2, supra, they are used to transfer territory, to regulate commercial relations, to settle disputes, to protect human rights, to guarantee investments, and so on.

The term "treaty", as used on the international plane, describes international agreements in general, whether they be denominated conventions, pacts, covenants, charters, protocols, etc. These different names have no legal significance; the same legal rules apply to one as to the other. The choice of this or that name may at times be prompted by the belief that a given designation implies greater or lesser solemnity or importance. But as a matter of international law, a treaty by whatever name is still a treaty. In U.S. domestic law, by contrast, the term "treaty" has a special meaning. It describes an international agreement that, unlike other agreements the U.S. might conclude, requires the advice and consent of the Senate before the U.S. may become a party to it. See generally, Chapter 8.

The international law of treaties has been codified to a large extent in the Vienna Convention on the Law of Treaties (1969). See generally, Sinclair, The Vienna Convention on the Law of Treaties (2d ed. 1984). The Convention entered into force in 1980 and has been ratified by many countries. Its authoritative character as law, even for states not parties to it, derives from the fact that it is now generally accepted to be declaratory of the customary international law of treaties. Although the U.S. has not become a party to the treaty, it considers that the substantive provisions of the Vienna Convention state the international law on the subject. See Restatement (Third), Part III, Introductory Note.

II. DEFINITION AND CONCLUSION OF TREATIES

§ 5–1. **Definition.** Treaties, whether bilateral or multilateral, are defined somewhat circuitously as agreements governed by international law. Since it is international law which applies to relations between and among the subjects of international law (states and intergovernmental organizations), it follows that agreements which they conclude with one another are, as a general rule, treaties. Some agreements entered into between states or international organizations may be governed, expressly or by implication, by domestic law and would, therefore, not be treaties but contracts. An example of such a contract would be an agreement between two states for the sale of land to construct an embassy that the parties intend to be governed by local property law. Other purely commercial arrangements (a contract for the sale of wheat or sugar, for example) between the governments of two or more states might fall into the same category. Although there is a presumption that an agreement between two states is a treaty, that presumption may be rebutted by a showing that they intended it to be governed exclusively by domestic law.

The Convention defines a treaty as "an international agreement concluded between States in written form and governed by international law . . .." Convention, art. 2(1)(a). This does not mean that an agreement between a state and an international organization or between two such organizations cannot be a treaty. See Convention, art. 3. The Convention adopts a more restrictive definition because it was expressly made applicable only to agreements between states. International agreements involving international organizations are governed by a more recent treaty, the Vienna Convention on the Law of Treaties between States and International Organizations or between International Organizations, which was adopted in 1986. 25 Int'l Leg.Mat. 543 (1986). This instrument complements the Vienna Convention on the Law of Treaties and amplifies to a significant extent the existing body of norms applicable to international agreements. Furthermore, although both of these Conventions apply only to written agreements, a treaty does not have to be in writing in order to be valid and enforceable under international law. See Legal Status of Eastern Greenland (Denmark v. Norway), 1933 PCIJ, ser. A/B, No. 53; Convention, art. 3.

§ 5–2. **Negotiation of treaties.** Although the same legal rules apply to multilateral and bilateral treaties, the process by which these treaties are negotiated and concluded may differ. Bilateral treaties tend to originate in the foreign ministry of one of the two interested parties. Following discussions, usually involving the respective embassies and exchanges of diplomatic notes, one or more draft texts will be prepared by the respective legal advisers. These texts will be the subject of negotiations until an acceptable draft has emerged.

Multilaterial treaties between only a few states tend to be negotiated much the same way as bilateral treaties. Treaties designed to have a large number of states parties are as a rule drafted at diplomatic conferences where the participating states are represented by diplomatic delegations that include legal advisers. The conference will usually have before it various working papers or draft proposals, prepared by some states or international organizations in advance of the meeting. These documents serve as the basis for the negotiations and bargaining that ultimately result in the text of a treaty. See Convention, art. 9.

The negotiating and drafting process at these diplomatic conferences resembles that of national legislatures. Here amendments to different provisions of the working papers are presented, rapporteurs are designated, drafting committees are established, alternative texts are proposed and debated, etc. The conference records are a valuable source of information on the drafting history of the treaty. The formal results of the conference are frequently summarized in a so-called Final Act, which usually contains the text of the treaty. The Final Act can and often does serve to authenticate the text of the treaty. See Convention, art. 10. But the adoption of the Final Act is not as a rule designed to bring the agreement into force.

§ 5–3. **Entry into force of treaties.** Bilateral treaties enter into force on the international plane when both states indicate their intention to be bound by the agreement as of a certain date. Multilateral treaties often contain a provision indicating how many states have to accept the treaty before it will be in force as between them. See Convention, art. 24.

§ 5–4. **Consent to be bound by treaty.** Article 11 of the Convention declares that "[t]he consent of a State to be bound by a treaty may be expressed by signature, exchange of instruments constituting a treaty, ratification, acceptance, approval or accession, or by any other means if so agreed." Under international law any of the abovementioned methods may be utilized by a state to indicate its acceptance of the treaty. Often, of course, the treaty will specify the method, and if it declares, for example, that the states will be bound upon signing the treaty, their signature will have that effect. Convention, art. 12.

It is more common for a treaty to provide that it shall become binding upon ratification. See Convention, art. 14(1). On the international plane, ratification is an act whereby a state, through its head of state, foreign minister, or duly authorized diplomatic agent, see Convention, art. 7, declares that it considers itself bound by the treaty. Convention, art. 14. The declaration is usually contained in a so-called instrument of ratification. These instruments are either exchanged between the parties or deposited with a previously designated depositary government or organization, which performs various custodial functions relating to the treaty. See Convention, arts. 76–77.

§ 5–5. **Signature followed by ratification.** If a treaty imposes a ratification requirement, it will most likely also provide for the prior signature thereof; ratification usually is the second step in a two-stage process, involving signature followed by ratification. In treaties which adopt this approach, the signature serves principally as a method for the authentication of the text of the agreement. Convention, art. 10. It is the states' subsequent ratification which brings the agreement into force for them; their earlier signature alone does not have that effect. By signing a treaty that is subject to ratification a state does not undertake to eventually ratify the agreement, although it does have some minimal obligations relating thereto. See Convention, art. 18.

Treaties tend to provide for signature followed by ratification in order to make it possible for governments to submit them to those national authorities, usually the legislatures, that are empowered under domestic law to approve the state's adherence to international agreements. Most national constitutions impose some such approval requirement, particularly for treaties that will have to be given effect on the domestic plane.

Treaties which call for signature and subsequent ratification usually also have a provision permitting accession. Such treaties might contain a provision that reads as follows, for example: "This treaty may be ratified by all states signatories thereto. Any other state wishing to become a party to it, may do so by depositing an instrument of accession [adherence]. . . ." Under such a clause, a signatory state becomes a party by ratification of the agreement; accession is reserved for states that were unable to or did not sign. Cf. Convention, art. 15. Once a state becomes a party, however, it matters not whether it did so by ratification, adherence, accession or any other method allowed under the treaty.

III. RESERVATIONS

§ 5–6. Definition. Article 2(d) of the Convention defines a reservation as follows:

> . . . a unilateral statement, however phrased or named, made by a State, when signing, ratifying, accepting, approving or acceding to a treaty, whereby it purports to exclude or to modify the legal effect of certain provisions of the treaty in their application to that State.

States sometimes sign and/or adhere to treaties with statements they label "reservations," "declarations," "understandings," "clarifications," etc. By defining a reservation as "a unilateral statement, however phrased or named," the Convention indicates that the label selected by a state will not be determinative. The test instead is whether the unilateral statement "purports to exclude or to modify the legal effect of certain provisions of the treaty in their application to that State." In that sense a reservation is an attempt by the reserving state to amend the treaty *pro tanto* the reservation as between itself and the other states parties to it.

An "understanding" or "declaration," by contrast, would be a statement in which a state declares that it understands a given provision of the treaty to mean "X", for example, without seeking the concurrence, either express or implicit, of any other state in the interpretation proposed by it.

To the extent that the state does not intend the "understanding" to have any legal effect as between itself and the other states, it will not be considered a reservation. In practice, there may be considerable ambiguity at times whether a declaration is a reservation or merely a unilateral interpretation, and some foreign offices will seek clarification to avoid subsequent misunderstandings.

States often attach understandings or other declarations to their ratifications because of domestic political or legal considerations. In states where domestic courts are called upon to apply and interpret international agreements, the formal interpretation of a treaty provision by their foreign offices or legislatures, however denominated, will carry great weight. And in some countries, the courts will consider themselves bound to give effect to these declarations, even though they may lack legal significance on the international plane.

§ 5–7. **The right to make reservations.** As a general rule, states are free to adhere to a treaty with reservations. There are three exceptions to this rule: if the treaty prohibits reservations, if the treaty permits only certain types of reservations and the one being made is of a different type or, in general, if the reservation is incompatible with the object and purpose of the treaty. Convention, art. 19. What types of reservations are incompatible with the object and purpose of the treaty is not always an easy question to answer. In a decision

bearing on this subject, the Inter-American Court
of Human Rights indicated that

> a reservation which was designed to enable a
> State to suspend any of the non-derogable funda-
> mental rights [guaranteed in the American Con-
> vention on Human Rights] must be deemed to be
> incompatible with the object and purpose of the
> [american] Convention . . ..

Advisory Opinion on Restrictions to the Death Penalty, I–A Court H.R., OC–3/83, ser. A, No. 3, para.
61; 23 Int'l Leg.Mat. 320 (1984). The Court based
this conclusion on the fact that the American Convention expressly barred states from suspending,
even in time of war or other national emergency,
the non-derogable rights referred to above. The
American Convention consequently attached the
greatest importance to the protection of these
rights, and to permit reservations that would remove these rights from the treaty would defeat
that overriding purpose. See also, Advisory Opinion on the Genocide Convention, 1951 ICJ 15, at
23–24.

§ 5–8. **Acceptance and legal effect of reservations.** A state's attempt to join a treaty with a
reservation constitutes a proposal to modify the
terms of the treaty as between it and the other
parties to the agreement. In the case of a bilateral
treaty, the acceptance of the reservation results in
an amendment of the treaty. If the treaty is
multilateral, the reservation will accomplish its
object only if at least some states are willing to

accept it. But if some states accept the reservation and others reject it, what treaty relations, if any, have been created? What acts constitute acceptance, and can acceptance be implied? Article 20 of the Convention deals with these and related questions.

First, a reservation expressly authorized by a treaty does not require acceptance. Convention, art. 20(1). See also, Advisory Opinion on the Effect of Reservations, I–A Court H.R., ser. A, No. OC–2/82, 22 Int'l Leg.Mat. 37 (1983). Second, some multilateral treaties, because of their special nature and the limited number of states that negotiated them, may indicate that a reservation requires acceptance by all parties. Convention, art. 20(2). Third, when a treaty is the constituent instrument of an international organization, the reservation will have to be accepted by the organization. Convention, art. 20(3).

In the circumstances described in the preceding paragraph, a state meeting the requisite requirements for the acceptance of its reservation becomes a party to the treaty. As between it and the other parties, the treaty will have been modified to the extent of the reservation. Convention, art. 21. But what is the law in situations where reservations are neither expressly prohibited nor expressly permitted, for example, and a state proposes to become a party with a reservation? If the reservation is not incompatible with the object and purpose of the treaty, the other states parties are free to accept or reject the reservation. Convention, art. 20(4). If the reservation has been accepted by a state party, the treaty will be in force as between it and the reserving state. Convention, art. 20(4) (a). As between a state party that objects to the reservation and the reserving state, the former has two choices. First, it may declare that it objects to the reservation and does not wish to enter into a treaty relation with the reserving state. As between these two states, there will be no treaty relation. Second, a party may refuse to accept the reservation but express no objection to entering into the treaty relation with the reserving state. Here it will be presumed that a treaty relation has been created. Convention, art. 20(4)(b).

When a reservation has been rejected by a state that did not object to the reserving state becoming a party to the treaty, the treaty will be in force as between them, but "the provisions to which the reservation relates do not apply as between the two States to the extent of the reservation." Convention, art. 21(3). In those cases where the reservation is either acceptable as a matter of law or has been accepted, the treaty is in force between the reserving state and the other parties, but their obligations are modified by the reservations. Convention, art. 21(1)(a). Of course, the reservation does not affect the treaty relations *inter se* the other states that became parties without a reservation. Convention, art. 21(2).

To illustrate the application of these rules, let us assume a multilateral treaty with a large number of states parties that contains no prohibition regarding reservations. Let us assume further that State A seeks to ratify with a reservation modifying article 5, paragraph 2, of the treaty. What will be the treaty relations of State A, if State B accepts the reservation, State C rejects it but does not object to A becoming a party, and State D objects to the reservation and does not want the treaty to enter into force between it and State A? Under the international law of treaties as codified in the Vienna Convention on the Law of Treaties, the result will be as follows: (1) between State A and B, the treaty is in force as modified by A's reservation to article 5(2); (2) between State A and C, the treaty is in force, but article 5(2) is inapplicable; (3) the treaty is not in force between A and D; (4) the treaty relations between B, C, D and all other parties and their obligations *inter se* are unaffected by A's reservation. The hypothetical would become more complicated if many of the other states parties themselves also made different types of reservations. This would further multiply the bifurcation of the treaty. That is, under the rules described above, reservations can and in fact do transform a multilateral treaty into a complex network of interrelated bilateral agreements.

IV. OBSERVANCE OF TREATIES

§ 5–9. Pacta sunt servanda. Article 26 of the
Convention declares that "[e]very treaty in force is
binding upon the parties to it and must be performed by them in good faith." The UN's International Law Commission, in its commentary to this
rule, characterized it as a "fundamental principle
of the law of treaties." 1966 Report of the ILC,
reproduced in 61 Am.J. Int'l L. 248, at 334 (1967).
The Restatement (Third) refers to this norm as
"perhaps the most important principle of international law." Id., Comment a. to § 321. Article 27
of the Convention makes clear, furthermore, that
the obligation to perform treaties in good faith
applies, as far as international law is concerned,
irrespective of any conflicting domestic law. It
provides that "[a] party may not invoke the provisions of its internal law as justification for its
failure to perform a treaty." See also, Convention,
art. 46. This, too, is an undisputed and fundamental principle of international law. See Chapter 1,
§ 1–9, supra.

§ 5–10. Territorial scope of treaties. Article
29 of the Convention provides that "[u]nless a
different intention appears from the treaty or is
otherwise established, a treaty is binding upon
each party in respect of its entire territory." Some
treaties contain federal-state clauses, which are
designed to permit federal states, which lack the
domestic legislative jurisdiction relating to a sub-

ject-matter dealt with by the treaty, to limit their obligations under the treaty to subjects within their federal jurisdiction. As article 29 indicates, such clauses may be permitted, but if they are not included in a treaty, a state party will not be able to deny the treaty's territorial scope even if it is a federal state, unless it makes an express reservation to that effect.

§ 5–11. **Interpretation of treaties.** Although at one time international legal scholars were divided about the law governing the interpretation of treaties, the applicable rules are today no longer in dispute. The basic principle is proclaimed in article 31(1) of the Convention, which stipulates that "[a] treaty shall be interpreted in good faith in accordance with the ordinary meaning to be given to the terms of the treaty in their context and in the light of its object and purpose." Hence, the starting point for the interpretation of an international agreement is the text, which is assumed to constitute "the authentic expression of the intentions of the parties." 1966 ILC Report, supra, at 354. In seeking to understand the terms used in the text, their "ordinary meaning" must serve as the guide. The Convention recognizes, however, that "[a] special meaning shall be given to a term if it is established that the parties so intended." Convention, art. 31(4). See Restatement (Third) § 325.

Article 31(2) defines the "context" as comprising, "in addition to the text, including its preamble and annexes," the following:

(a) any agreement relating to the treaty which was made between all the parties in connexion with the conclusion of the treaty;

(b) any instrument which was made by one or more parties in connexion with the conclusion of the treaty and accepted by the other parties as an instrument related to the treaty.

The basic principle here is that the treaty must be interpreted as a whole. In seeking to understand the meaning of a treaty provision, for example, it is not enough to look only at the text of the particular provision. It must be analyzed in a manner that relates the specific contents of the provision to the object and purpose of the treaty as reflected in its text and those additional instruments that are referred to in article 31(2). The preamble can often be particularly relevant when one seeks to determine the object and purpose of the agreement.

The Convention also recognizes that subsequent agreements between the parties regarding the interpretation or application of the treaty as well as subsequent relevant practice by them "shall be taken into account, together with the context," in interpreting a treaty. Convention, art. 31(3). The drafting history or so-called *travaux preparatoires* of a treaty is characterized as a "supplementary means of interpretation." Convention, art 32. Recourse to it may be had only in two circumstances: first, to "confirm" the meaning derived from the textual analysis; second, when the textual analysis "(a) leaves the meaning ambiguous or obscure; or (b) leads to a result which is manifestly absurd or unreasonable." Ibid.

§ 5–12. **Treaties and third states.** It is a basic principle of international treaty law that "a treaty does not create either obligations or rights for a third State without its consent." Convention, art. 34. Under certain circumstances, however, third states can assume obligations and be granted rights under treaties to which they are not parties. The latter situation would be true, for example, if the treaty conferred third-party beneficiary status on a non-state party. See Convention, arts. 35–36. These rules should not be confused with the principle that the norms enunciated in a treaty can become binding on states that are not parties to it. That principle applies only in situations where the law codified in the treaty is or has become customary international law. Convention, art. 38. See generally, Chapter 2, supra.

V. INVALIDITY, TERMINATION AND SUSPENSION OF TREATIES

§ 5–13. **Invalidity of treaties.** The usual grounds which may be invoked under domestic law to invalidate contracts, that is, error of fact, fraud, corruption and duress, are also available under international law to invalidate treaties. See Convention, arts. 48–52. Moreover, a treaty is void *ab initio* if, at the time it was entered into, it was in conflict with a peremptory norm of general international law (*jus cogens*). Convention, art. 53. Although domestic law contains many provisions of law and public policy that are obligatory in the sense that individuals may not by contract enter into arrangements in conflict with them, the basic assumption in international law is almost absolute freedom of contract. In general, states are free to enter treaties that change, as between them, otherwise applicable rules of customary international law. The only limitation on that right is a rule of law having the status of *jus cogens;* that is, states may not by treaty contravene a rule of *jus cogens*.

The Convention defines "a peremptory norm of general international law" as follows: "a norm accepted and recognized by the international community of States as a whole as a norm from which no derogation is permitted and which can be modified only by a subsequent norm of general international law having the same character." Convention, art. 53. The Convention does not identify any such norms, and there is little overall agreement on the subject. It seems to be generally accepted, however, that a treaty to commit genocide or to legalize the slave trade, for example, would be void as in contravention of *jus cogens*. See generally, Frowein, "Jus Cogens," in Encyclopedia of Public International Law, Instalment 7, at 327 (Bernhardt ed. 1984). Finally, it should be noted that a treaty, valid at the time of its conclusion, will become void if it conflicts with a *jus cogens* norm that has emerged subsequently. Convention, art. 64.

§ 5–15 *INVALIDITY, ETC.* 109

§ 5–14. Domestic law and invalidity. States sometimes attempt to avoid performing their obligations under a treaty by claiming that their consent to be bound by the treaty was invalid because it was effected in a manner that violated applicable domestic law. This argument will fail unless the "violation was manifest and concerned a rule of . . . [the state's] internal law of fundamental importance." Convention, art. 46(1). The Convention clarifies the matter further by providing that "[a] violation is manifest if it would be objectively evident to any State conducting itself in the matter in accordance with normal practice and in good faith." Convention, art. 46(2). Here it might be asked, for example, whether the failure of the President of the U.S. to submit a treaty to the Senate for its advice and consent before ratifying the agreement would permit the U.S. to declare its consent invalid? The answer has to be no, because under U.S. law there are a number of different types of international agreements which the President may ratify with or without the Senate's advice and consent. The law on that subject is by no means clear. See Chapter 8, § 8–5, infra. At times, in fact, the President may decide to seek the Senate's consent when he might have chosen a different route, and vice versa. In the light of these circumstances, the violation would certainly not be manifest to a foreign state. See Restatement (Third), § 311, Comment c.

§ 5–15. Termination, suspension and breach of treaties. The mere fact that the government of a state party to a treaty has changed or has been overthrown, does not as a matter of law terminate or result in the suspension of the treaty. The same is true if the parties to the treaty sever diplomatic or consular relations. Convention, art. 63. Of course, a treaty may be suspended if it can be shown that it was tied specifically to the existence of a particular government or if diplomatic or consular relations are indispensable for its application.

States may withdraw from a treaty, terminate it or suspend its operation in a manner prescribed by the treaty or with the consent of all states parties thereto. Convention, arts. 54 and 57. Treaties usually contain provisions permitting withdrawal subject to certain notice requirements, but even where the treaty does not contain a specific clause on the subject, the right to denounce may be implied under certain circumstances. See Convention, art. 56.

It is an established principle of international law that a material breach of a treaty is a valid ground for its suspension or termination. A material breach has traditionally been defined as "the violation of a provision essential to the accomplishment of the object or purpose of the treaty." Convention, art. 60(3)(b). The unlawful repudiation of the treaty in its entirety, of course, also constitutes a material breach. Convention, art. 60(3)(a).

The Convention distinguishes between the material breach of a bilateral treaty and of a multilater-

al one. Convention, art. 60. In the case of the
former, it declares that "[a] material breach of a
bilateral treaty by one of the parties entitles the
other to invoke the breach as a ground for termi-
nating the treaty or suspending its operation in
whole or in part." Convention, art. 60(1). If a
multilateral treaty has been materially breached
by a party, a distinction has to be made between
the rights of all other (innocent) parties to the
treaty, on the one hand, and states parties specially affected. Convention, art. 60(2). The latter
have the right to suspend, but not to terminate, the
operation of the treaty in whole or in part in
relation to the defaulting state. Convention, art.
60(2)(b). The former have the right to suspend or
terminate the treaty altogether or only as between
themselves and the defaulting party, provided the
decision to do so has been arrived at by unanimous
agreement of the innocent parties. Convention,
art. 60(2)(a). See Restatement (Third) § 335.

The rules which the Convention prescribes for
the suspension or termination of treaties because
of a material breach are made expressly inapplicable "to provisions relating to the protection of the
human person contained in treaties of a humanitarian character, in particular to provisions prohibit-
ing any form of reprisals against persons protected
by such treaties." Convention, art. 60(5). Treaties
of a humanitarian character are the 1949 Geneva
Conventions and the 1977 Protocols thereto, for
example, which deal with the treatment of prison-

ers of war, the protection of civilians, and wounded military personnel, etc. A material breach by one party to these treaties does not authorize the other to suspend their operation in relation to the individuals they seek to protect even if they are nationals of the defaulting state. See Advisory Opinion on the Effect of Reservations, I–A Court H.R., OC–2/82, ser. A., No. 2, 22 Int'l Leg.Mat. 37 (1983), which analyzes the unique character of humanitarian and human rights treaties and the consequences it has on questions relating to the interpretation and application of treaties.

International law recognizes that a fundamental change of circumstances (*rebus sic standibus*) and impossibility of performance may in certain situations justify the termination of or the withdrawal from a treaty. Impossibility of performance may be so invoked, for example, if "the impossibility results from the permanent disappearance or destruction of an object indispensable for the execution of the treaty." Convention, art. 61(1). This will not be a valid ground for termination or withdrawal by the party invoking it "if the impossibility is the result of a breach by that party either of an obligation under the treaty or of any other international obligation owed to any other party to the treaty." Convention, art. 61(2).

A fundamental change of circumstances, which was not foreseen by the parties, will justify termination of or withdrawal from a treaty only if

(a) the existence of those circumstances constituted an essential basis of the consent of the parties to be bound by the treaty; and

(b) the effect of the change is radically to transform the extent of obligations still to be performed under the treaty. Convention, art. 62(1). See Fisheries Jurisdiction Case (U.K. v. Iceland), 1973 ICJ 3.

But even if the above two conditions are met, this ground may not be invoked to terminate or withdraw from a treaty if the treaty establishes a boundary. It may also not be resorted to if the changed circumstances resulted from a violation by the state invoking it of an international obligation under the treaty or any other international obligation owed to any of the parties to the treaty. Convention, art. 62(2). Of course, the grounds that a state may invoke to terminate a treaty or to withdraw from it because of impossibility of performance or changed circumstances also permit the less serious remedy of suspension. See Convention, arts. 61(1) and 62(3). See generally, Restatement (Third) § 336.

The effect of war or other armed hostilities on treaties is a subject that was expressly excluded from the Convention. Id., art. 73. As a practical matter, most treaties are suspended, if not terminated, in wartime. Cf. Techt v. Hughes, 229 N.Y. 222, 128 N.E. 185 (1920), cert. denied, 254 U.S. 643 (1920). This is, of course, not true with regard to treaties that are intended to be applied in wartime situations, for example, treaties relating to the law of war and humanitarian treaties. Furthermore, various human rights treaties contain provisions that prohibit the suspension even in wartime of certain of the most basic rights that the treaties guarantee. See International Covenant on Civil and Political Rights, art. 4; European Convention of Human Rights, art. 15; American Convention on Human Rights, art. 27. In the past, it was customary for peace treaties to include an agreed upon list of pre-war treaties deemed to continue in force.

It is important to recognize that states frequently invoke the various grounds referred to in this section in order to justify the suspension or termination of and their withdrawal from a treaty, even when there is little or no valid basis for doing so. To limit these abuses, the Convention establishes a formal procedure that must be followed by states asserting the right to terminate or withdraw from a treaty on these grounds. Convention, arts. 65–68.

CHAPTER 6

THE RIGHTS OF INDIVIDUALS

I. INTRODUCTION

This chapter deals with the international law that applies to the protection of the human rights of individuals. On this subject generally, see Buergenthal, International Human Rights in a Nutshell (1988). The law on this subject evolved from two different branches of international law: the international law of human rights and the law on the international responsibility of states for injuries to aliens. Although the substantive rights that each of these branches protects can be said to have converged in recent decades, significant procedural distinctions exist between them, depending upon the particular branch in which the rights are sought to be enforced. This chapter will therefore deal separately with the law of state responsibility and the international law of human rights.

These two branches of the law differ in one major respect: the law of state responsibility protects individuals against violations of their rights only when their nationality is not that of the offending state; international human rights law protects individuals regardless of their nationality. The concept of nationality is irrelevant in human rights law because the individual is deemed to be the subject of these rights. Nationality is of vital importance, however, under the law of state responsibility because here the injury to a national is deemed to be an injury to the state of his/her nationality. This legal fiction accommodates the traditional doctrine that individuals are not subjects of rights under international law. See generally, Case Concerning the Barcelona Traction, Light and Power Company, Limited (Belgium v. Spain), 1970 ICJ 3. Hence, if an individual is stateless or a national of the offending state, any remedy he/she might have on the international plane would have to be found in the international law of human rights and not that of state responsibility.

II. INTERNATIONAL LAW OF HUMAN RIGHTS

§ 6–1. **Historical development.** The international law of human rights evolved over the last four decades, tracing its origin to the adoption of the Charter of the United Nations. This is not to say that prior to 1945 there existed no rules that would today be deemed to be part of the international law of human rights. What did not exist prior to 1945 was a comprehensive body of law that protected the individual *qua* human being. The international law of the pre-UN Charter era did, however, develop various rules and institutions that today are part of the international law of human rights. See generally, Sohn, "The New

International Law: Protection of the Rights of the Individual Rather Than States," 32 Am.U.L.Rev. 1, 2–6 (1982).

The doctrine of humanitarian intervention, which deals with the right of states and international organizations to come to the assistance of the nationals of a state if it subjects them to treatment that "shocks the conscience of mankind," can be traced back to Grotius. See generally, Sohn and Buergenthal, The International Protection of Human Rights 137–43 (1973). International agreements to combat the slave trade originated in the early decades of the 19th century. The treaties that sealed the Peace of Westphalia (1648), see Chapter I, § 1–16, dealt with some aspects of religious freedom in Europe, as did the Treaty of Paris (1856) and the Treaty of Berlin (1878).

The peace treaties that ended the First World War (1914–1918) established a formal system for the protection of national, religious and linguistic minorities under the administration of the League of Nations, which applied in various parts of Central, Eastern and Southeastern Europe. See Sohn and Buergenthal, supra, at 213. The Covenant of the League of Nations created the so-called Mandate system. It applied to certain colonial territories that were placed under the protection of the League, which had the task of ensuring that the states administering these territories would promote the welfare of the native populations. See

Advisory Opinion on Namibia, 1971 ICJ 16. During that same period, the International Labor Organization began the process of promoting international standards for the protection of workers. International efforts making some basic humanitarian norms applicable to the conduct of war gained formal multilateral recognition as early as 1864. The law applicable to the responsibility of states for the injuries to aliens, which can be traced back to the early days of modern international law, is yet another precursor of international human rights law. Although it protects only foreign nationals, it produced a body of human rights law binding on all states and universal in character. See Restatement (Third), Part VII, Introductory Note.

A. The Law of the UN Charter

§ 6–2. The United Nations Charter. What distinguishes the human rights provisions of the UN Charter from earlier international agreements or from preexisting customary international law on the subject is their general scope. The pre-Charter human rights law was designed to protect certain categories of human beings or to guarantee certain types of rights. The Charter imposes no such limitations. It speaks of "human rights and fundamental freedoms for all without distinction as to race, sex, language or religion." UN Charter, art. 55(c). See also, id., arts. 1(3), 13(1)(b) and 62(2).

The Charter creates two interrelated obligations. It provides, first, that the UN "shall promote . . .

universal respect for, and observance of, human rights and fundamental freedoms for all without distinction as to race, sex, language or religion." UN Charter, art. 55(c).   Second, it contains a pledge by the member states of the UN "to take joint and separate action in cooperation with the Organization for the achievement of the purposes set forth in Article 55."   UN Charter, art. 56.   The commitment to promote human rights and fundamental freedoms was thus established as a legally binding obligation both of the Organization and of its member states.   Modern international human rights law has its source in these two provisions. They laid the conceptual foundation for the development of substantive human rights law and for making human rights a matter of international concern.

§ 6–3. **The Universal Declaration of Human Rights.**   The UN Charter speaks only of "human rights and fundamental freedoms" without defining or enumerating them.   The principal instrument to perform these functions is the Universal Declaration of Human Rights, which was proclaimed by the UN General Assembly on December 10, 1948.   Although adopted in the form of a nonbinding resolution, the Universal Declaration has over the years come to be accepted as an authoritative interpretation or definition of the rights that the UN and its member states have an obligation to promote under articles 55 and 56 of the UN Charter.   Various commentators have argued, furthermore, that it has acquired the status of customary international law. Much more general support exists for the view that at least some of the rights proclaimed in the Universal Declaration enjoy the status of customary international law, including freedom from systematic governmental acts and policies involving torture, slavery, murder, prolonged arbitrary detention, disappearances, racial discrimination, and other gross violations of human rights. See, e.g., Filartiga v. Pena-Irala, 630 F.2d 876 (2d Cir.1980); Restatement (Third) § 702. There is also support for the proposition that a state which pursues a governmental policy denying individuals or groups the rights proclaimed in the Declaration because of their race, sex, language or religion, violates the principle of non-discrimination that is fundamental to the human rights obligations assumed by the states parties to the UN Charter.

The Universal Declaration proclaims a catalog of basic civil and political rights, including the right to life, the right not to be held in slavery, not to be tortured, to equal protection of law, to due process guarantees, freedom of speech, assembly and movement, the right to privacy, etc. It also guarantees the right to own property as well as a number of economic, social and cultural rights, such as the right to work, to education, to health care and various other social services, and to participate in the cultural life of the community. All of these rights are proclaimed in language that is general in character and lacking the specificity of a treaty or law. The Declaration does recognize, however, that states may limit the rights it proclaims by laws intended to secure "due recognition and respect for the rights and freedoms of others and of meeting the just requirements of morality, public order and the general welfare in a democratic society." Universal Declaration, art. 29(2).

§ 6–4. **The UN Human Rights Covenants.** In 1966, the UN General Assembly adopted the International Covenant on Civil and Political Rights, the International Covenant on Economic, Social and Cultural Rights, and the Optional Protocol to the Civil and Political Covenant. These instruments, together with the Universal Declaration and the human rights provisions of the UN Charter, comprise what is known as the "International Bill of Human Rights." See generally, Robertson, Human Rights in the World 24 (2d ed. 1982); Buergenthal, International Human Rights in a Nutshell 24–47 (1988).

The Covenants are treaties requiring ratification. They entered into force in 1976 after ratification by thirty-five states, the number prescribed to bring them into effect. That number has in the meantime increased very substantially. The U.S. is not a party to the Covenants, although it signed them and President Jimmy Carter referred them to the Senate for its advice and consent to ratification.

In addition to proclaiming two so-called rights of peoples—the right to self-determination and the right of all peoples to freely dispose of their natural wealth and resources—the Covenant on Civil and Political Rights guarantees a large number of individuals rights and freedoms. See generally, Henkin (ed.), The International Bill of Rights (1981); Meron, Human Rights Law-Making in the United Nations 83 (1986). The list includes, *inter alia,* the right to life, freedom from torture and slavery, the right to liberty and security of person, the right of detained persons to be treated humanely, the right not to be imprisoned for debt, freedom of movement, the right to a fair trial, freedom from *ex post facto* laws and penalties, the right to privacy, freedom of thought, opinion, expression, conscience and religion, freedom of assembly and association, the right to marry and found a family, the rights of the child, the right to participate in government, and equal protection of law. The right to property, proclaimed in the Universal Declaration, does not appear in either Covenant.

The Covenant on Civil and Political Rights is drafted with much greater legal precision than is the Universal Declaration. The rights are qualified, moreover, by various exceptions, restrictions and limitations. A special provision, permitting the suspension of some rights in emergency situations, is also included. Civil and Political Covenant, art. 4.

The Covenant on Economic, Social and Cultural Rights amplifies the list of rights that the Universal Declaration proclaims on this subject. It also guarantees the same rights of peoples established in the Civil and Political Covenant. The principal difference between these two instruments, apart from the rights they ensure, is that they impose different legal obligations. The ability to guarantee many of the economic, social and cultural rights proclaimed in the Covenant on that subject presupposes the availability of economic and other resources that not all states dispose of to the same extent. Few such resources are required, as a general rule, in order for states to comply with their obligations to protect civil and political rights; more often than not, they are obliged merely to abstain from acting in a manner that violates these rights. These considerations explain why the states parties to the Covenant on Economic, Social and Cultural Rights merely undertake to take steps "to the maximum of [their] available resources" to achieve "progressively the full realization of the rights recognized in the . . . Covenant by all appropriate means, including particularly the adoption of legislative measures." Id., art. 2(1). The Covenant on Civil and Political Rights, by contrast, requires each state party to undertake "to respect and to ensure to all individuals within its territory and subject to its jurisdiction the rights" recognized in that Covenant. Id., art. 2(1). Here the obligation to comply is immediate, whereas the states parties to the Covenant on Economic, Social and Cultural Rights assume an obligation that is progressive in character and tied to the availability of resources.

The so-called measures of implementation, that is, the international methods for the supervision of compliance by the states parties with their obligations under the respective Covenants also differ significantly. The Covenant on Civil and Political Rights, supplemented by the Optional Protocol, provides for a system, albeit quite weak, that permits investigation and quasi-adjudication of individual and inter-state complaints by a committee of experts. It also reviews the periodic reports of the member states. Although the Covenant on Economic, Social and Cultural Rights provides only for a system of periodic reports to be filed with the Economic and Social Council of the UN, that body has now established a special Committee on Economic, Social and Cultural Rights. This committee is composed of 18 experts who are elected in their individual capacities. Its function is to review the reports that the states parties and the specialized agencies are required to provide to the ECOSOC pursuant to the provisions of the Covenant. See generally, Alston, "Out of the Abyss: The Challenges Confronting the New U.N. Committee on Economic, Social and Cultural Rights," 9 Hum. Rights Q. 332 (1987).

§ 6-5. **Other UN human rights instruments.** The International Bill of Human Rights is supplemented by a large number of human rights treaties concluded within the framework or under the auspices of the UN. Most important of these are the Genocide Convention (1948), the International Convention on the Elimination of All Forms of Racial

Discrimination (1965), the Convention on the Political Rights of Women (1953), and the International Convention on the Suppression and Punishment of the Crime of Apartheid (1973). All of these human rights treaties have entered into force and some of them, the Genocide Convention and the Racial Convention, for example, have been ratified by the vast majority of UN member states. The U.S. has ratified only the Convention on the Political Rights of Women and the Genocide Convention.

§ 6–6. The specialized agencies and regional organizations. The specialized agencies of the UN, particularly the International Labor Organization and UNESCO, have coordinated their codification efforts in the human rights area with those of the UN and adopted many treaties and other instruments on the subject. Three regional international organizations—the Council of Europe, the Organization of American States, and the Organization of African Unity—have established treaty-based regional systems for the protection of human rights, which were inspired in large measure by the Universal Declaration and other UN human rights efforts. See this Chapter, part II.B, infra. See also, Weston, Lukes & Hnatt, "Regional Human Rights Regimes: A Comparison and Appraisal," 20 Vand.J. Transl L. 585 (1987).

§ 6–7. The international human rights code and its legal effect. The treaties described in the preceding sections and numerous other international agreements that were not mentioned for lack of space have created a vast body of international human rights law. See Lillich (ed.), International Human Rights Instruments (1983). The parties to these treaties are legally bound, of course, to comply with the obligations they have assumed thereunder. A more difficult question concerns the obligation of the states that have ratified the UN Charter and only some or a few of the other agreements. To the extent that multilateral international agreements can be the source of general or customary international law, see Chapter 2, supra, UN human rights practice can create and has created international human rights law. The primary source of that law is the UN Charter and the Universal Declaration, reinforced by the large body of existing conventional law, by the resolutions and other acts of international organizations, and by the practice of states.

The proposition that there has emerged a body of general international human rights law is today no longer seriously disputed with regard to some of the most fundamental rights, which outlaw genocide, torture and slavery, and other large-scale violations of human rights. See Restatement (Third), § 702. See also, Filartiga v. Pena–Irala, 630 F.2d 876 (2d Cir.1980). There is greater uncertainty with regard to violations involving rights of lesser magnitude that are guaranteed in all or some of these treaties. Few areas of international law have experienced and continue to experience as much legislative activity as has the human rights field. This ongoing law-making process, which proceeds at a relatively rapid pace, contributes to the uncertainty regarding specific rights.

An equally important effect of the human rights provisions of the UN Charter and the legislative practice described above concerns the internationalization of human rights. Prior to the Second World War, human rights issues were, in general, not regulated by international law and, therefore, deemed to be matters within the domestic jurisdiction of each state. The manner in which a state treated its own nationals was, with some exceptions, not a matter of international concern and, hence, an issue that other states had no right to address on the international plane. Today, the manner in which a state treats its nationals is no longer *ipso facto* a matter within its domestic jurisdiction. As a general proposition, the contrary is no doubt true because such a large body of international law applies to human rights. Thus, for example, it would not be intervention in the domestic affairs of a state for another state to express concern about or to ask the former to explain large-scale violations of internationally recognized human rights. Contemporary international law does not prohibit such intrusion. See Henkin, "Human Rights and 'Domestic Jurisdiction'," in Human Rights, International Law and the Helsinki Accord 21 (Buergenthal ed. 1977).

B. Regional Human Rights Law and Institutions

1. The European System

§ 6–8. **The European Convention of Human Rights.** Drafted within the framework of the Council of Europe, the European Convention of Human Rights entered into force in 1953. More than 20 Western European countries have to date ratified the Convention, including all member states of the European Common Market. The Convention, as originally adopted, protected only a dozen fundamental civil and political rights. This catalog of rights has been substantially expanded with the entry into force of various Additional Protocols to the Convention, which are used by the states parties to add new rights to the protected categories. The right to property, for example, became a right guaranteed in the Convention with the entry into force of the first Protocol in 1954. See generally, Van Dijk & van Hoof, Theory and Practice of the European Convention on Human Rights (1984); Fawcett, The Application of the European Convention on Human Rights (2d ed. 1987).

§ 6–9. **The Convention Institutions.** The Convention established the most advanced international system for the protection of human rights in existence today. It consists of the European Commission of Human Rights and the European Court of Human Rights. Together with the Committee of Ministers of the Council of Europe, these two institutions supervise the enforcement of the rights which the Convention guarantees. The Commission has 21 members, its size being determined by the number of states parties to the Convention. The size of the Court corresponds to the membership of the Council of Europe, which now stands at 22 member states. See European Convention of Human Rights [hereinafter European Convention], arts. 20 and 38.

The Commission has jurisdiction to hear interstate and individual petitions. Its jurisdiction to deal with a case filed by one state against another state is compulsory as soon as both states have ratified the Convention. European Convention, art. 24. The Commission's jurisdiction to decide individual petitions is optional. That jurisdiction may be invoked only if the state, in addition to ratifying the Convention, has made a declaration accepting the right of the Commission to hear cases brought against it by individuals. European Convention, art. 25. To date most states have filed the requisite declaration.

The Court's jurisdiction is optional. By ratifying the Convention, a state is not deemed to have accepted the Court's jurisdiction; a special declaration to that effect by the state concerned is necessary. European Convention, art. 46. Most states have made such a declaration. Only states and the Commission may refer cases to the Court. Individuals have no standing to do so. The Court's judgments are final and binding. European Convention, arts. 52 and 53. In addition to its power to decide whether or not a state party has violated the Convention, the Court has the power also to award damages to the injured party. European Convention, art. 50.

§ 6–10. **Enforcing the rights guaranteed.** An individual who considers himself to be a victim of a violation of a right that the Convention guarantees must exhaust all available domestic remedies before the case may be filed with the Commission. European Convention, art. 26; Lawless v. Ireland, 2 Yearbook of the European Convention of Human Rights [hereinafter yearbook] 308 (1958–59). The Commission deals with a case in three basic stages. First, it passes on the admissibility of the case, which involves a determination whether the petition states a *prima facie* case and whether the available domestic remedies have been exhausted. European Convention, art. 27. If the case is determined to be inadmissible, it proceeds no further and no appeal is possible. The second stage begins if a case has been ruled admissible. Here the Commission seeks to ascertain the facts and to assist the parties in reaching a friendly settlement. If no such settlement can be achieved, the Commission prepares a report containing its findings of fact and its opinion as to whether the facts disclose a violation of the Convention. European Convention, arts. 28–31. This report must be referred to the Committee of Ministers of the Council of Europe. (The Committee, which is the policymaking organ of the Council, consists of government representatives of the member states of the Council.) The third stage begins with the transmission of the report to the Committee of Ministers. Within a period of three months of that transmission, the Commission or any interested state party may refer the case to the Court, provided it has jurisdiction to hear the matter. European Convention, arts. 32(1) and 48. If the case has not been submitted to the Court, it can be decided only by the Committee of Ministers. European Convention, art. 32.

A case that has gone to the Court can be heard by it in a chamber consisting of seven judges or by the full Court, depending upon the overall importance of the issues presented. Although the individual victim who has initiated the proceedings before the Commission cannot take the case to the Court, he/she has the right to be heard by and to be represented before the Court. See European Court of Human Rights, Revised Rules of Court, arts. 30 and 33. The execution of the Court's judgments is supervised by the Committee of Ministers. European Convention, art 54.

Since its establishment in 1959, the Court has rendered numerous judgments finding states parties to be in violation of their obligations under the Convention and requiring them to pay compensation. The record of compliance by the states has been excellent; in only one case has the implementation of a judgment been delayed, and it involved difficult political and constitutional issues. See

Belgian Linguistic Case, 9 Yearbook 832 (1968). For an analysis of the case law of the European Court and Commission, see Higgins, "The European Convention on Human Rights," in Human Rights in International Law: Legal and Policy Issues 495 (Meron ed. 1984). See also, Merrills, The Development of International Law by the European Court of Human Rights (1988).

2. *The Inter-American System*

§ 6–11. **The two sources of the system.** The inter-American system for the protection of human rights has two distinct legal sources. One is the Charter of the Organization of American States, the other source is the American Convention on Human Rights. The institutions of this system have a different history and different powers depending upon whether they were established pursuant to the Charter or the Convention. See generally, Buergenthal, "The Inter-American System for the Protection of Human Rights," in Meron, supra, at 439. It is useful, therefore, to treat them separately.

§ 6–12. **The OAS Charter system.** In 1960, based on some very general references to human rights in the 1948 OAS Charter, the OAS established the Inter-American Commission on Human Rights. (See Chapter 3, supra, for a description of the OAS.) The Commission, created as an "autonomous entity" of the OAS under a Statute adopted by the OAS Council, was charged with the task of promoting the human rights that the American

Declaration of the Rights and Duties of Man proclaims. That Declaration was adopted in 1948 in
the form of a non-binding OAS conference resolution. When the OAS Charter was amended in
1970, the Commission became an OAS Charter
organ. See OAS Charter, as amended, art. 51(e)
[now art. 52(e)]. The amendment strengthened the
constitutional authority and legal powers of the
Commission and, by necessary implication, the normative status of the American Declaration. OAS
Charter, as amended, arts. 112 [now art. 111] and
150; Buergenthal, "The Revised OAS Charter and
the Protection of Human Rights," 69 Am.J.Int'l L.
828 (1975).

These and related developments establish that a
member state of the OAS that has not ratified the
American Convention on Human Rights is deemed
to have an OAS Charter obligation to promote the
human rights that the American Declaration proclaims. Statute of the Inter-American Commission
on Human Rights, art. 1(2)(b). The power to ensure compliance with that obligation rests with the
Inter-American Commission on Human Rights
and, ultimately, the OAS General Assembly. In
discharging this mandate, the Commission receives
individual communications, prepares country studies, and undertakes on-site investigations. To this
end, it has prepared country studies and reports on
the human rights situations in various states, including Argentina, Chile, Cuba, Guatemala, Nicaragua, and Paraguay, among others. The publica-

tion of these reports and their review by the political organs of the OAS have on a number of occasions had a significant impact and resulted in an improvement of conditions in some of these countries. See generally, Medina, The Battle of Human Rights: Gross, Systematic Violations and the Inter-American System (1988).

When the Commission acts pursuant to its OAS Charter mandate, it may investigate human rights conditions in any OAS member state without having to await formal inter-state or individual complaints. Statute of the Inter-American Commission on Human Rights, arts. 18 and 20. This power has proved to be of great value for the protection of human rights in the inter-American system, permitting speedy intervention that would not be possible under the more formal system established by the Convention.

§ 6–13. The Convention system. The American Convention on Human Rights entered into force in 1978 and has been ratified by 20 out of the 31 OAS member states. The U.S., Brazil, Chile and Paraguay are among the states that have thus far not ratified it; all other major countries of the region have done so. See Buergenthal, "The U.S. and International Human Rights," 9 Hum.Rights L.J. 141 (1988).

The American Convention was modelled on the European Convention and resembles the latter in its institutional structure. The American Convention guarantees some 22 basic civil and political rights.   Unlike its European counterpart, the American Convention contains a federal-state clause, which enables some federal states to assume more limited territorial obligations than those incumbent on unitary states. See American Convention, art. 28.

The American Convention establishes an Inter-American Commission on Human Rights and an Inter-American Court of Human Rights. Both bodies consist of seven members, the former elected by the OAS General Assembly, the latter by the states parties to the Convention. See American Convention, arts. 36 and 53. This difference in the selection process of the judges of the Court and the members of the Commission is explained by the fact that the same Commission acts both as the OAS Charter organ referred to in the preceding section and as Convention organ. Thus, all OAS member states have an interest in the Commission's composition. The Court does not perform a comparable function.

The principal function of the Commission under the Convention is to deal with communications charging violations of the rights the treaty guarantees.   American Convention, arts. 41(f), 44–51. The Convention is unique among international human rights instruments in making the right of individual petition mandatory and that of interstate communications optional. American Convention, arts. 44–45. That is to say, as soon as a state has ratified the Convention, the Commission has jurisdiction to deal with an individual petition directed against that state. A state may file a complaint against another state only if both of them, in addition to ratifying the Convention, have accepted the Commission's jurisdiction to receive inter-state applications.

The Court has contentious and advisory jurisdiction. American Convention, arts. 62 and 64. Under its contentious jurisdiction, the Court has the power to decide cases involving charges that a state party has violated the rights guaranteed in the Convention. This jurisdiction is optional and must be accepted by the states parties before cases may be filed by and against them. Only the Commission and the states may bring cases to the Court; individuals lack standing to do so. American Convention, art. 61.

The Court's advisory jurisdiction authorizes it to render opinions interpreting the Convention and other treaties dealing with the protection of human rights in the inter-American system. Convention, art. 64. That jurisdiction, which may be invoked by all OAS member states, whether or not they have ratified the Convention, and by all OAS organs, is more extensive than the advisory jurisdiction of any international tribunal in existence today. See Advisory Opinion on "Other Treaties," Inter-American Court of Human Rights, Sept. 24, 1982, 22 Int'l Leg.Mat. 51 (1983); Advisory Opinion on the Death Penalty, Inter-American Court of Human Rights, Sept. 8, 1983, 23 Int'l Leg.Mat. 320

(1984); Advisory Opinion on Habeas Corpus in Emergency Situations, OC–8/87, Inter-American Court of Human Rights, Series A: Judgments and Opinions, No. 8 (1987).

§ 6-14. **Enforcing the Convention.** The American Convention, unlike its European counterpart, confers standing on individuals and organizations generally, even if they are not the victims of the violation complained of, to bring the violation to the attention of the Commission. American Convention, art. 44. To be admissible, however, all available domestic remedies must have been exhausted in the case. American Convention, art. 46. It must also meet various other admissibility criteria, including the requirement that the complaint state a *prima facie* case. American Convention, art. 47. There is no appeal from a rejection by the Commission of a communication at the admissibility stage.

Once a case has been admitted, the Commission investigates the facts and attempts to negotiate a friendly settlement. American Convention, art. 48. If a friendly settlement has not been achieved, the Commission prepares a report which is transmitted to the parties to the dispute, containing findings of fact and recommendations. Convention, art. 50. If within a three-months period following the transmission of the report the Commission's recommendations are not accepted or the case has not been referred to the Court, the Commission has the power to make a final determination in the matter and to set deadlines within which the defendant state must adopt the measures indicated by the Commission. American Convention, art. 51. See Godinez Cruz Case (Prel. Objections), Inter-American Court of Human Rights, Series C: Decisions and Judgments, No. 3 (1987).

The case may be referred to the Court by the Commission and by the states parties to the Convention, provided the states concerned have accepted the Court's jurisdiction. American Convention, art. 61. The Convention is unclear whether any state party which has accepted the Court's jurisdiction may do so, even if it did not participate in the proceedings before the Commission. The issue remains to be decided by the Court. What is clear, however, is that a case may only be dealt with by the Court under its contentious jurisdiction if the Commission proceedings in the matter have run their normal course. See American Convention, art. 61(2); In the Matter of Viviana Gallardo (Costa Rica), Inter-American Court of Human Rights, Decision of Nov. 13, 1981, No. G101/81, Series A: Judgments and Opinions 11 (1984); 20 Int'l Leg. Mat. 1424 (1981). The judgments of the Court are final and binding on the parties. American Convention, art. 67–68. Besides having the power to award damages and render declaratory decrees, the Court may in certain special circumstances also enter preliminary injunctions. See American Convention, arts. 63 and 68.

In the first few years of its existence—it was established in 1979—the Court's judicial practice consisted almost entirely of advisory opinions. See Buergenthal, "The Advisory Practice of the Inter-American Court of Human Rights," 79 Am.J.Int'l L. 1 (1985). The only exception was the *Viviana Gallado* case, supra, which was a highly unusual litigation. Here Costa Rica sought to seize the Court with jurisdiction of a complaint that had as yet not been filed by anyone against that government, bypassing the proceedings before the Commission. The Court dismissed the case on the ground that it lacked jurisdiction. In 1986, the Commission referred three so-called "disappearance" cases to the Court. These have now been decided. To date, they have produced three judgments dealing with jurisdictional issues and three adjudicating the merits. Velasquez Rodriguez Case (Prel. Objections), Judgment of June 26, 1987, I.–A. Court H.R., Series C: Decisions and Judgments, No. 1; Fairen Garbi and Solis Corrales Case Case (Prel. Objections), Judgment of June 26, 1987, ibid., No. 2; Godinez Cruz Case (Prel. Objections), Judgment of June 26, 1987, ibid., No. 3; Velasquez Rodriguez Case (Merits), Judgment of July 29, 1988, ibid., No. 4; Godinez Cruz Case, Judgment of January 20, 1989, ibid., No. 5; Fairen Garbi and Solis Corrales Case, Judgment of March 17, 1989, ibid., No. 6. See also, Gros-Espiell, "Contentious Proceedings Before the Inter-American Court of Human Rights," 1 Emory J. Int'l Disp.Res. 175 (1987).

3. The African System

§ 6–15. The African Charter of Human and Peoples' Rights. This treaty was adopted in 1981 by the Organization of African Unity and entered into force in 1986. Africa thus becomes the third region in the world with its own human rights system. More than 30 OAU member states have to date ratified the Charter, making it the largest such system in existence today. See generally, Bello, "The African Charter on Human and Peoples' Rights: A Legal Analysis," in Hague Academy, 194 Recueil des Cours 12 (1985). See also, International Commission of Jurists, Human and Peoples' Rights in Africa and the African Charter (1985).

§ 6–16. The Charter institutions. The African human rights system differs in a number of respects from the two other regional systems described in the preceding sections. The African Charter does not provide for the establishment of a human rights court. It does, however, create an African Commission on Human and Peoples' Rights with power to deal with inter-state and individual petitions. See African Charter, arts. 47–57. The full scope and meaning of this power remains to be defined by the practice of the Commission. It is worth noting, in this connection, that the Charter places much greater emphasis on friendly settlement and negotiations to resolve charges of violations of human rights than the instruments in force in Europe and in the Americas. See Gittleman, "The African Commission on Human Rights and Peoples' Rights: Prospects and Procedures," in Guide to International Human Rights Practice 153 (Hannum ed. 1984).

§ 6–17. The rights guaranteed. As for the rights it guarantees, the Charter draws heavily on the UN Covenants on Human Rights, although it weakens these rights with provisions that permit the imposition of far-reaching restrictions and limitations. See, e.g., African Charter, art. 6. The Commission has been given broad interpretative power, however, which might enable it over time to narrow the scope of these restrictions and limitations. African Charter, art. 45. This power is amplified by article 60 of the Charter, which authorizes the Commission, in interpreting the Charter, to "draw inspiration from international law on human and peoples' rights." That law is described in article 60 by reference to "the provisions of various African instruments on human and peoples' rights, the Charter of the United Nations, the Charter of the Organization of African Unity, the Universal Declaration of Human Rights . . ." as well as other OAU and UN instruments. It is much too early to say how this provision and the Charter itself will be applied. See generally, Gittleman, "The African Charter on Human and Peoples' Rights: A Legal Analysis," 22 Va.J.Int'l L. 667 (1982).

C. International Humanitarian Law

§ 6–18. **Definition and sources.** International humanitarian law can be defined as the international law of human rights that is applicable in situations of international armed conflict and, to a much more limited extent, in some situations of internal armed conflict. It might also be defined as the human rights component of the law of war. See generally, Kalshoven, Constraints on the Waging of War (1987).

Some humanitarian law has its source in customary international law and in various treaties relating to the law of war adopted at the Hague Peace Conferences of 1899 and 1907. The principal sources of this law, however, are the four Geneva Conventions of 1949, which entered into force in 1950, and the two Protocols Additional to these Conventions, which entered into force in 1978. See generally, Dinstein, "Human Rights in Armed Conflict: International Humanitarian Law," in Meron, supra, at 345. The U.S. has ratified the Conventions, but it is not a party to the Protocols.

§ 6–19. **The Geneva Conventions.** These treaties consist of the Geneva Convention for the Amelioration of the Condition of the Wounded and Sick in Armed Forces in the Field; the Geneva Convention for the Amelioration of the Condition of the Wounded, Sick, and Shipwrecked Members of Armed Forces at Sea; the Geneva Convention relative to the Treatment of Prisoners of War; and the Geneva Convention relative to the Protection

of Civilian Persons in Time of War. Some 150
states are parties to these treaties, making them,
together with the UN Charter, the most widely
ratified international agreements dealing with
human rights issues.

The Geneva Conventions apply in two very distinct circumstances. With one notable exception,
the four Conventions apply to armed conflicts between two or more of the states parties to these
treaties. See Geneva Convention, art. 2 (common
art. 2). That is, they apply to and in international
armed conflicts, imposing humanitarian rules for
the treatment of prisoners of war, wounded and
disabled members of the armed forces, whether on
land or sea, and the civilian populations. Only one
provision—the so-called common article 3—lays
down rules applicable to conflicts "not of an international character occurring in the territory" of
one of the states parties.

The distinction between an international and
non-international armed conflict is not always easy
to make, particularly in civil war situations involving contested claims of foreign intervention. See
Gasser, "Internationalized Non-International
Armed Conflicts: Case Studies of Afghanistan,
Kampuchea, and Lebanon," 33 Am.U.L.Rev. 145
(1983). Equally difficult to ascertain in practice is
the threshold for the application of common article
3. The dispute here usually involves the question
when a situation may be validly characterized as a
conflict "not of an international character," which

would make article 3 applicable, rather than a minor internal disturbance to which the Geneva Conventions would not apply. See, e.g., Goldman, "International Humanitarian Law and the Armed Conflicts in El Salvador and Nicaragua," 2 Am.U.J.Int'l L. & Pol. 539 (1987).

Many contemporary conflicts involve large-scale internal armed insurgencies that may not qualify as international armed conflicts. Here common article 3 of the Geneva Conventions is often the only applicable humanitarian law provision. Article 3 requires the parties to the conflict—the government and the insurgents—to treat "humanely" all "persons taking no active part in the hostilities, including members of armed forces who have laid down their arms and those placed *hors de combat* by sickness, wounds, detention, or any other cause . . . ." Adverse distinctions in treatment based "on race, colour, religion or faith, sex, birth or wealth, or any other similar criteria" are prohibited. Also prohibited are the following acts:

(a) violence to life and person, in particular murder of all kinds, mutilation, cruel treatment and torture;

(b) taking of hostages;

(c) outrages upon personal dignity, in particular, humiliating and degrading treatment;

(d) the passing of sentences and the carrying out of executions without previous judgment pronounced by a regularly constituted court, affording all judicial guarantees which are recognized as indispensable by civilized peoples.

Article 3 requires, furthermore, that "the wounded and sick . . . be collected and cared for." It also permits the International Committee of the Red Cross to offer its humanitarian services to the parties to the conflict. Although the guarantees spelled out in article 3 are not very extensive, they provide some protection in circumstances where any humane treatment, however elementary, amounts to progress.

§ 6–20. **The Protocols additional to the Geneva Conventions.** These two treaties, popularly known as Protocol I and Protocol II, supplement the four Geneva Conventions. See generally, Bothe, Partsch & Solf, New Rules for Victims of Armed Conflicts (1982). Each is designed to serve a different function: Protocol I applies, in general, to international armed conflicts and Protocol II to internal conflicts. Protocol II amplifies and clarifies the protection provided for in common article 3 of the Geneva Conventions. Protocol I does that in part as well because it applies not only to international conflicts within the meaning of common article 2 of the Geneva Conventions, but also to "armed conflicts in which peoples are fighting against colonial domination and alien occupation and against racist régimes . . .." Protocol I, art. 1(4). Thus, to the extent that an internal armed conflict comes within this latter definition, to that extent the parties to the conflict are required to accord the individuals concerned the additional rights and protection they would otherwise enjoy only if the conflict were international in character. See, e.g., Protocol I, art. 75.

§ 6–21. **Human rights conventions, derogation, and humanitarian law.** The major international human rights instruments in force today contain so-called derogation clauses, which permit the states parties to suspend, in time of war or other national emergency, certain of the rights guaranteed by these treaties. See Covenant on Civil and Political Rights, art. 4; European Convention of Human Rights, art. 15; American Convention on Human Rights, art. 27. The right of derogation is limited, however, in two very important respects. First, all derogation clauses list certain fundamental rights that may not be suspended under any circumstances. Second, they provide that, even with regard to the rights that are suspendable, the measures which the states parties may take in emergency situations must not be "inconsistent with [their] . . . other obligations under international law." See, e.g., American Convention, art. 27(1).

The reference to other international obligations has important consequences. For a state party to one of the aforementioned human rights treaties, which has also ratified the Geneva Conventions and the two Protocols, the humanitarian law agreements would be deemed incorporated by reference into the derogation clause of the human rights treaty and bar any derogation inconsistent with the humanitarian law conventions. Moreover, certain measures not prohibited by the Geneva Conventions or the Protocols in time of war or national emergency could not be lawfully adopted by a state party to the human rights treaty, if such measures violated a human right that was nonderogable under the treaty. See generally, Meron, Human Rights in Internal Strife: Their International Protection (1987).

III. STATE RESPONSIBILITY FOR INJURIES TO ALIENS

§ 6–22. Historical development. Whereas the international law of human rights has a very recent history, the basic principles of the law of state responsibility for injuries to aliens can be traced to the early days of modern international law. These principles were amplified and refined by international arbitral tribunals in the 19th and early 20th centuries and to a lesser extent by the Permanent Court of International Justice.

The relevant law can be divided into two parts: the procedural law of state responsibility and its substantive counterpart. The latter relates to the content of the law, that is, to the legal rights and obligations that it creates. The procedural law deals with the manner in which these rights and obligations are enforced. Although the relevant procedural law is today quite clear, considerable uncertainty exists about the content of some substantive norms.

A. Procedural Issues

§ 6–23. **The nationality requirement.** The law of state responsibility for injuries to aliens can only be invoked on the international plane by a state whose national is alleged to be a victim of a violation of that law. On nationality, see Chapter 7, infra. For the purpose of asserting a claim, the injury, if there be any, is deemed to be an injury to the state of the alien's nationality. Panevezys-Saldutiskis Railway (Judgment), 1939 PCIJ, ser. A/B, No. 76; Mavrommatis Palestine Concessions (Jurisdiction), 1924 PCIJ, ser. A, No. 2. Hence, if the alien is a stateless person, has the nationality of the state alleged to have acted wrongfully or, although formally a national of the espousing state, his/her nationality is not entitled to recognition on the international plane, the claim will have to be dismissed. Nottebohm Case (Liechtenstein v. Guatemala), 1955 ICJ 4. If an individual has dual nationality, either state of his/her nationality may file a claim against a third state. The former may not, however, sue each other because either state is free to treat the individual as its national. Mergé v. Italian Republic, 1955, 14 UN Rep.Int'l Arb. Awards 238. But see, Esphahanian v. Bank of Teherat, Iran-U.S. Claims Tribunal, 78 Am.J.Int'l L. 914 (1984).

Claims under the law of state responsibility may be asserted also on behalf of juridical persons such as corporations. A state espousing the claim of a corporation will have to show that the corporation has its nationality. That question is usually determined by reference to the entity's place of incorporation and/or its principal place of business *(siège social)*. Case Concerning the Barcelona Traction, Light and Power Company, Limited (Belgium v. Spain), Second Phase, 1970 ICJ 3.

§ 6–24. **Exhaustion of domestic remedies.** Before a state may espouse a claim on behalf of its national, it must be shown that the latter has exhausted all available legal remedies in the courts and before the administrative agencies of the state against which the claim is brought. The Interhandel Case (Switzerland v. United States), 1959 ICJ 6. This requirement is designed to permit a state to remedy a wrong at the domestic level before it is converted into a dispute on the international plane, where it might unnecessarily disrupt relations between states. It should be noted, in this connection, that the exhaustion of domestic remedies is also a requirement found in various international human rights instruments. Today there exists a vast body of law and practice on this subject, most of it developed in the context of human rights complaints but equally applicable to state responsibility cases. See generally, Trindade, The Application of the Rule of Exhaustion of Local Remedies in International Law (1983).

The exhaustion of domestic remedies requirement may be waived by the state against which the claim is lodged. De Wilde, Ooms and Versyp v. Belgium, Judgment of June 18, 1971, European Court H.R.Publs, ser. A, No. 12 (1971). It is also excused if it can be established that it would be futile to resort to domestic remedies or because none are in fact available. Velasquez Rodriguez Case (Prel. Objections), I-A. Court H.R., Series C: Decisions & Judgments, No. 1 (1987). See García-Amador, Sohn and Baxter, Recent Codification of the Law of State Responsibility for Injuries to Aliens 261–76 (1974). International tribunals will not readily presume the unavailability of domestic remedies unless the relevant evidence is over-whelming.

§ 6–25. **Presentation and settlement of claims.** After a claimant has failed to obtain satisfaction in the state alleged to have violated his/her rights, the claim may be espoused by the state of the claimant's nationality. The decision whether to espouse the claim is a political question within the discretion of each individual state.

Once the claim has been espoused, it takes on an international character in the sense that it be-comes the subject of international negotiations be-tween the state of the claimant's nationality and the state against which the claim is asserted. Sometimes the claim is settled at this stage. If this does not happen, the states concerned might decide to litigate it either in an international arbi-tral tribunal or in the International Court of Jus-tice. Sometimes, too, states will negotiate a lump sum settlement of all outstanding claims or decide to submit the claims to special arbitral tribunals. The Iran-U.S. Claims Tribunal is a recent example of an arrangement of the latter type. See Stewart and Sherman, "Developments at the Iran-United States Claims Tribunal: 1981–1983," 24 Va.J.Int'l L. 1 (1984); Lillich and Weston, International Claims: Their Settlement by Lump Sum Agreements (1975). Some claims, though, may never be satisfactorily resolved. On the methods available to states seeking to obtain satisfaction, see Oliver, "Legal Remedies and Sanctions," in International Law of State Responsibility for Injuries to Aliens 61 (Lillich ed. 1983).

When a claim has been espoused by a state, it has the right under international law to waive the claim, to settle it, and, in all respects, to control the negotiations or litigation relating to it. Moreover, the funds a state receives in satisfaction of a claim are deemed under international law to belong to the state receiving them. Domestic law may require a state to pay the money to the individual claimant, but international law does not impose that requirement. Some states, including the U.S., have from time to time established national commissions to adjudicate the claims of their nationals to a share of the funds comprising the lump sum settlement. See Lillich, International Claims: Their Adjudication by National Commissions (1962); Restatement (Third) § 713 Reporters' Notes 9.

In order to prevent international claims from being brought against them on behalf of foreign nationals, some states have sought to force foreigners, as a condition of doing business within their territories, to waive the right to seek diplomatic protection from their home states. Provisions requiring such waivers have been included in domestic legislation or concession contracts, particularly in Latin America. These "Calvo clauses," named after the Argentine diplomat and scholar who proposed them, have been held by international tribunals to be incapable of depriving the state of the alien's nationality of the right to espouse a national's claim if the individual's rights under international law were violated. Cf. North American Dredging Co. v. United Mexican States, General Claims Comm'n (U.S.-Mexico), 1927, 44 UN Rep. Int'l Arb. Awards 26. The theory of these holdings is that the right of diplomatic protection belongs to the state and not to the claimant. See generally, García-Amador, Sohn and Baxter, supra, at 291–94.

B. Substantive Aspects

§ **6–26. Attributable liability.** A state is liable under international law for an injury to a foreign national only if the wrongful act or omission is attributable to it. Under this principle, a state is responsible for the conduct of its government organs, agencies or officials, acting within the scope of their authority or under color of such authority. It matters not whether the agencies or officials belong to the national government or to local governmental entities. See Restatement (Third), § 207.

As a general rule, the private acts of individuals will not be treated as state action unless the state has encouraged such action or fails to take reasonable measures to protect the aliens. Failure to punish persons who have injured an alien or refusal to permit redress in local courts may implicate the state. A state may also become responsible for private acts by ratifying them. See Case Concerning United States Diplomatic and Consular Staff in Teheran (United States v. Iran), 1980 ICJ 3; Laura Janes Claim (United States v. Mexico), General Claims Comm'n, 1926, 4 UN Rep.Int'l Arb.Awards 82; Garcia and Garza Claim (Mexico v. United States), id., at 119.

§ **6–27. Scope of liability.** Under traditional international law, states were deemed to be liable for official acts or omissions involving a "denial of justice" falling below the "international minimum standard." The phrase "denial of justice" was sometimes applied only to violations committed by the judicial authorities of the states, at other times it was used to describe all wrongful acts attributable to a state. The test for determining whether an act or omission was wrong was the so-called "international minimum standard." Some states, notably those of Latin America, contended that aliens were entitled to no more and no less than "national treatment," which meant that as long as an alien was not discriminated against, he/she had no right to receive better treatment than nationals.

Although the international minimum standard came to be accepted as the test applicable to state responsibility claims, its substantive content remained an issue of considerable controversy. See e.g., the separate opinions in Chattin Claim (United States v. Mexico), General Claims Comm'n, 1927, 4 UN Rep.Int'l Arb.Awards 282. The arbitral tribunals could point to few principles of customary international law on the subject and, therefore, relied mainly on general principles of law derived from national legislation and court decisions when deciding what constituted a denial of justice. Some states viewed these principles as European standards of justice that were imposed on them without regard for domestic legal and political realities.

With the adoption of the Universal Declaration of Human Rights and other instruments dealt with in part II of this Chapter, the debate has lost much of its significance. These instruments supply an international standard that has been developed and accepted by the international community for the treatment of all human beings, regardless of the nationality they might have. This is also the view of the Restatement (Third), which in § 711 declares that a state is responsible for injuries incurred by foreign nationals that were caused by official acts or omissions violating internationally recognized human rights. See also Restatement (Third) § 701.

Of course, a state is also liable for violations of treaties for the protection of the rights of foreign nationals residing in its territory. Many treaties exist today which guarantee a variety of civil, economic and other rights to certain aliens. See, e.g., Swendig v. Washington Water Power Co., 265 U.S. 322 (1924); Avigliano v. Sumitomo Shoji America, Inc., 638 F.2d 552 (2d Cir.1981). Some rights, furthermore, may be entitled to protection under international law even though they are not "internationally recognized human rights" or embodied in treaties. See Restatement (Third), § 711(b) and (c). This is particularly true in the area of economic rights.

§ **6–28. Economic rights.** Claims for the infringement of economic rights usually involve either expropriation of property or the cancellation of or interference with an alien's contract or concession agreement. While it is clear that a nation may take alien-owned property located within its borders as an incident of its sovereignty, substantial controversy exists about whether and, if so, how much compensation is required when such a taking occurs. The capital exporting countries have adopted the position that expropriation is lawful only if there is a public purpose for the taking and it is not in retaliation against the alien in question because of his nationality or to apply in a discriminatory manner. These states argue that "full compensation" is required whenever a taking occurs. Most Communist countries contend that a state may expropriate the means of production at any time for any purpose with whatever compensation it decides is appropriate. Treaties between these countries do provide, however, for payment of compensation for the taking of property belonging to each other's nationals. The less developed countries appear to have taken a middle course, acknowledging the right of a state to expropriate foreign-owned property but recognizing a requirement of "just" or "appropriate" compensation, defined in the light of all the circumstances surrounding the taking, including the purpose of the taking and the expropriating state's ability to pay. A somewhat more restrictive attitude is reflected in the Charter of Economic Rights and Duties of States, adopted by the UN General Assembly in 1974 by a vote of 120 to 6 with 10 abstentions. That Charter declares a right in each state

to nationalize, expropriate or to transfer ownership of foreign property, in which case appropriate compensation should be paid by the State adopting such measures, taking into account its relevant laws and regulations and all circumstances that the State considers pertinent. In any case where the question of compensation gives rise to controversy, it shall be settled under the domestic law of the nationalizing State and by its tribunals . . . [unless otherwise agreed].

This provision would deny the relevance of international law as a source for defining standards for compensation. But see Texaco Overseas Petroleum v. Libyan Arab Republic, 17 Int'l Leg.Mat. 1 (1978).

There is a dispute also over whether contractual rights and concession agreements should be accorded the same treatment as rights in tangible property when the value of those rights is impaired or nullified by state action. The mere breach of a contract by a state does not raise international legal liability unless the breach is accompanied by an abuse of governmental power, e.g., failure to permit access to local courts to try the issue of breach. On the other hand, the arbitrary nullification of a contract or concession agreement is deemed to be a violation of international law.

According to the Restatement, a taking of property will be unlawful under international law if it is not for a public purpose, is discriminatory or if "just compensation" is not paid. Restatement (Third), § 712. The Restatement defines "just compensation" as "fair market value" except in very exceptional circumstances. As a practical matter, in the majority of international dispute settlements, the traditional measure of compensation as set forth in the Restatement has been applied, i.e., that compensation must be an amount equivalent to the value of the property taken and must be paid at the time of the taking, or with interest from that date, and in a form economically usable by the foreign national. Ibid. This conclusion is reflected in provisions of recent bilateral investment treaties and in friendship, commerce and navigation treaties, as well as in decisions of the Iran-U.S. Claims Tribunal. See, e.g., Starret Housing Corp. v. Islamic Rep. of Iran, 23 Int'l Legal Mat. 1090 (1984); American Int'l Group v. Islamic Rep. of Iran, 23 Int'l Legal Mat. 1 (1983); Kuwait v. American Independent Oil Co., 21 Int'l Legal Mat. 976 (1982); Sedco v. National Iranian Oil Co., 25 Int'l Leg.Mat. 629 (1986).

CHAPTER 7

JURISDICTION

I. INTRODUCTION

This chapter treats principles of jurisdiction
found in customary international law and applied
in courts in the United States. These principles
determine (a) the authority of a state to adjudicate
the rights of particular parties in its courts or
other agencies, (b) the authority of a nation to
establish the norms of conduct that shall be applicable to events or persons inside or outside its
borders and (c) the authority of the state to exercise power to compel conduct in obedience to its
appropriately prescribed norms. Traditionally,
types of jurisdiction were characterized under two
headings: jurisdiction to prescribe norms of conduct and jurisdiction to enforce the norms prescribed. §§ 17–20, Restatement (Second) Foreign
Relations Law of the U.S. (1965). The Restatement
(Third) adopts a tri-partite characterization: jurisdiction to prescribe, jurisdiction to enforce and
jurisdiction to adjudicate. See § 401, Restatement
(Third).

The scope of a state's jurisdiction over given
persons or events is a function of the interest of
that state in affecting the subject in question.
That interest is determined by the quality and

quantity of linkages that exist between the state
and those persons or events. Concurrent jurisdiction may exist under international law because
more than one nation may have legitimate interests in prescribing, adjudicating or enforcing with
respect to the same events or persons. Most U.S.
courts use principles of international comity to
determine how the exercise of concurrent authority shall be coordinated or the conflict resolved.
The Restatement (Third) concludes that where concurrent jurisdiction exists and two or more states
have issued conflicting prescriptions for conduct,
international law requires each state to balance its
interests against those of the other state or states
involved. A state with weaker interests is encouraged, but not required, to defer to the exercise
of jurisdiction by another state having stronger
interests. See Restatement (Third), § 403(3). In
the United States, international jurisdictional principles become applicable by means of the legal
fiction that the law-maker, usually the legislature,
will be presumed to intend that the law operate
within these principles unless the intent of the
law-maker to violate them is absolutely clear. The
Charming Betsy, 6 U.S. (2 Cranch) 64, 118 (1804);
See United States v. Aluminum Co. of America,
148 F.2d 416, 443 (2d Cir.1945). Additionally, a
series of U.S. Supreme Court cases has emphasized
that jurisdictional decisions should be grounded on
principles likely to further and encourage the development of an effective international system.
See Maier, "Extraterritorial Jurisdiction at a

Crossroads: An Intersection Between Public and Private International Law," 76 Am.J.Int.L. 280, 303–316 (1982).

II. INTERNATIONAL JURISDICTIONAL PRINCIPLES

§ 7–1. **The Lotus Case.** The principal judicial statement of these principles in customary international law is the opinion in the *S.S. Lotus Case,* (France v. Turkey), 1927 PCIJ, ser. A, No. 10. In that case, France objected to Turkey's attempt to try a French naval lieutenant for criminal negligence that caused a collision between his ship and a Turkish vessel on the high seas, killing several Turkish citizens. In its ruling on jurisdiction, the PCIJ concluded that Turkey was free to act unless a customary prohibition against the exercise of jurisdiction could be found. After stating that territorial jurisdiction was a fundamental element of the sovereignty principle in the international legal system, the Court wrote:

Far from laying down a general prohibition to the effect that States may not extend the application of their laws and the jurisdiction of their courts to persons, property, and acts outside their territory, it leaves them in this respect a wide measure of discretion which is only limited in certain cases by prohibitive rules; as regards other cases, every State remains free to adopt the principles which it regards as best and most suitable. Id.

The Court concluded: "All that can be required of a State is that it should not overstep the limits which international law places upon its jurisdiction; within these limits, its title to exercise jurisdiction rests in its sovereignty." Id. at 19.

Building upon this concept, the *Harvard Research in International Law,* 29 AJIL Supp. 435 (1935), identified five principles that had been asserted to support jurisdiction: the nationality principle, the territoriality principle, the protective principle, the universality principle and the passive personality principle. The most current statement of these principles is found in Restatement (Third) Foreign Relations Law of the U.S. (1987), §§ 401–404. The first three are generally supported by international custom, the fourth is accepted for special situations while the last is generally disfavored. Thus, a state has jurisdiction over all acts committed by its nationals, over all acts occurring within its territory, and over all acts occurring outside its territory that threaten its security as a state or certain other state interests. Restatement (Third), § 402. It also has jurisdiction to punish acts such as piracy that are universally recognized as being a threat to the community of nations no matter where those acts take place. Restatement (Third), § 404. Normally, the state whose national is injured by an act will not have jurisdiction over the act that caused the injury or the person committing it solely because the injured person was a national of the state claiming jurisdiction. Restatement (Third), § 402, comment (g). Although these principles are designed to describe the scope of a state's jurisdiction in criminal matters, they apply also when states attempt to regulate commercial or other conduct outside their borders, even though that regulation does not include criminal penalties.

§ 7–2. The nationality principle.　States have jurisdiction over their nationals, even when those nationals are physically outside the country's borders. This is so both because the national owes allegiance to his own country no matter where he or she is located and because each nation has both responsibility to other nations for the conduct of its nationals and an interest in their welfare while they are abroad.

§ 7–3. Nationality. a. *Persons.* Each state has the right to define who are its nationals. Nationality may be acquired "naturally" as the result of birth, either by being born within a state's territory (*jus soli*) or through the nationality of one's parents (*jus sanguinis*) or both. It may also be acquired "artificially," by naturalization. Naturalization can occur by voluntary application and acceptance in a formal process or as the result of marriage, adoption or redintegration—the reacquisition of an original nationality by operation of law. An individual may also become a national of a state that acquires the territory on which he lives.

Although traditionally relationships between a state and its nationals are not matters subject to international law, assertion of jurisdiction based on nationality over a person or corporation also claimed as a national by another state raises the question of which state may appropriately make that claim. In certain circumstances, it is possible for a person to be treated as having dual nationality. Normally, the consent of an individual is required before a state can confer its nationality upon that person.

A state must have a reasonable connection with a person to claim him or her as a national even when that individual consents. For a state validly to claim jurisdiction based on nationality there must be a genuine link between the state asserting jurisdiction on that basis and the person or entity over whom jurisdiction is asserted. Nottebohm (Liechtenstein v. Guatemala), 1955 ICJ 4. The quantity and quality of the connections required to establish effective nationality depend upon the facts of each case; but in every instance, the assertion must be reasonable in light of the circumstances. In certain situations, especially with relationship to private law matters such as domestic relations issues, international law recognizes that a state may exercise jurisdiction over non-nationals on the basis of residence or domicile. See Restatement (Third), § 402, comment e. This derives from a combination of national interests reflected in the nationality and territoriality principles.

b. *Corporations.* A corporation has the nationality of the state that creates it. Barcelona Traction Light and Power Co., Ltd., (Belgium v. Spain), 1970 ICJ 3, 168; Restatement (Third) For.Rel.Law, § 213. The connection provided by the act of creation is sufficient to permit a state to exercise jurisdiction over a corporation under the nationality principle. Whether a state may treat a corporation that is *not* incorporated under its laws as its national is unclear. A genuine link must exist between the state asserting nationality and the corporation subject to the claim. Restatement (Third), Sec. 211, comment (c). Among such links are the nationality of owners of a substantial number of the corporation's shares, location of the corporate management office (called the *siège social* or corporate seat in some continental corporate codes) or the location of a principal place of business. See Restatement (Third), § 213, comment (d). In certain circumstances—e.g. where the corporation is in fact only a corporate shell—it may be treated as having the nationality of its shareholders for limited purposes. In some circumstances, a state may exercise jurisdiction over foreign branches of domestically organized corporations by virtue of its jurisdiction over the parent or home office as long as that attempted exercise is reasonable. See Restatement (Third) § 414(1) and comment c; § 403(2).

c. *Vessels.* A state has jurisdiction over vessels flying its flag. S.S. Lotus, PCIJ (1927), supra.

This jurisdiction is often described by the fiction that the vessel is part of the territory of that state. Actually, jurisdiction over vessels is based on a theory akin to the nationality principle. A ship has the nationality of the state in which it is registered, regardless of the nationality of the owner or the crew. A nation is the sole judge of whether registration of a ship under its laws is appropriate but whether such registration will be recognized externally is determined by the international community. Some nations, especially those in the "Panlibhon Group"—Panama, Liberia and Honduras—permit ship registry with few prerequisites except the payment of a fee. This fact led to the creation of "flags of convenience," (also called "open registry operations"), registration of ships having little or no connection with the country of registry to take advantage of favorable maritime regulatory regimes.

In modern times, flags of convenience have been challenged on the grounds that a "genuine link" must exist between the ship and the nation whose flag it flies, applying by analogy, the rule in *Nottebohm,* supra, to ships. Restatement (Third), § 501. Article 5 of the 1958 Convention on the High Seas adopted the genuine link rule and added that the state of registry had a duty to exercise jurisdiction over ships registered to it. The Convention contained no provisions, however, indicating the consequences of registration when no genuine link existed. Both the requirement and the omission are repeated in Article 91 of the Law of the Sea Convention. A state's assertion of the right to extend diplomatic protection to a vessel may be rejected by another state if the asserting state has no genuine link with the vessel in question. Restatement (Third), Sec. 501, comment b. United States courts have held that United States maritime regulatory legislation will apply to ships registered in other countries when those ships have significant contacts with the United States. Hellenic Lines, Ltd. v. Rhoditis, 398 U.S. 306 (1970).

d. *Aircraft and spacecraft.* The same general rules that determine the nationality of vessels apply to aircraft under the 1944 Chicago Convention on International Civil Aviation. Spacecraft are subject to the jurisdiction of the state that registers them under Article 8 of the Treaty on Principles Governing the Activities of States in the Exploration and Use of Outer Space, Including the Moon and Other Celestial Bodies. This treaty does not use the characterization "nationality" but rather allocates "jurisdiction and control" to the registering state.

§ 7–4. The territorial principle. A state has absolute, but not necessarily exclusive, power to prescribe, adjudicate and enforce rules of law for conduct that occurs within its own territory. It may also act to affect interests in a *res* or the status of persons located within its territory. Restatement (Third), § 402(1). This authority is based on a "pure" territoriality principle. It reflects the community recognition that without the power to control acts or things located in its territory, a state could not exist; and that other nations must be able to rely on the state's territorial authority to fix the territorial sovereign's responsibility to protect their rights and interests within its territory. Thus, the territorial principle serves both to limit state authority and to distribute competence among international community members. The Island of Palmas Case (Netherlands v. United States), 2 R.Int.Arb. Awards 829, 839 (1928).

In addition, a state has jurisdiction to prescribe, adjudicate or enforce rules of conduct for acts that occur outside its territory but which have effects within it. This "objective territoriality" principle was recognized in the *S.S. Lotus Case, (France v. Turkey)*, supra, when the Court ruled that acts of criminal negligence occurring aboard a French ship on the high seas could be adjudicated and punished under Turkish law because the negligence had caused effects within Turkish jurisdiction. The Court wrote:

[o]ffenses, the authors of which at the moment of commission are in the territory of another State, are nevertheless to be regarded as having been committed in the national territory, if one of the constituent elements of the offense, and more especially the effects, have taken place there. Id. at 38.

This theory recognizes that without the authority to regulate foreign-based acts that have domestic effects, a nation would be powerless to protect its citizens and residents, a *sine qua non* of statehood. Its principal and most controversial applications are to support the assertion of jurisdiction to regulate foreign-based activities that have or threaten adverse economic effects within the regulating state. The objective territoriality theory is related to the development of an international nuisance doctrine under which a state is responsible to another for permitting its territory to be used in such a way as to create harm in the latter's territory. The Trail Smelter Arbitration (United States v. Canada), 3 U.N.Rep.Int.Arb.Awards 1911 (1941).

§ 7–5. **Territorial jurisdiction.** Territorial jurisdiction includes not only the territorial sovereign's exclusive right to carry out the activity within its defined territory but the correlative duty to protect the rights of other states and their nationals within that territory. Island of Palmas Case, supra, at 839. Control over territory is an essential element of state sovereignty. Therefore, a state necessarily has jurisdiction to prescribe, apply and enforce its law as to conduct occurring within its territory. Originally, those areas that a state could in fact control—land territory and contiguous waters and airspace—were subject to its jurisdiction. Modern weaponry and technology make this test obsolete. Today, international legal limitations on a state's jurisdictional authority are not coextensive with the state's physical power to enforce its will but reflect appropriate accommodations of national and community interests in preserving an orderly international regime.

a. *Land boundaries.* A state's land boundaries are normally determined by either express or tacit agreement with its neighbors on a case by case basis. Thus, there is no general customary rule for determining boundaries. One exception is, however, a customary rule of international law that fixes boundaries in navigable rivers at the "thalweg", the middle of the navigation channel. Other internal water boundaries are at the center of the bordering body of water. § 12(2) Restatement (Second) For.Rel.L. (1965).

b. *Territorial waters.* The international law delineating national jurisdiction over contiguous ocean space has had a long historical development. During the 18th century, the width of a state's territorial sea was generally agreed to be the length of a cannon shot. During the nineteenth century a three mile limit to territorial waters came to be accepted by most states, due in part to the impracticality of changing the breadth of territorial waters to reflect improvements in land-based artillery. After World War I, acceptance of the three-mile limit became less general. Neither the 1958 nor the 1960 Geneva conference on the law of the sea could reach agreement on an acceptable limit. Currently, twelve miles appears to be generally accepted with some states claiming additional territorial waters or "patrimonial seas" up to 200 miles in breadth. In addition to territorial waters, states have also claimed limited jurisdictional rights in contiguous zones to protect the adjacent territorial sea, in fisheries zones in which they claim jurisdiction to regulate fishing activity and in submarine areas in which they claim jurisdiction over minerals and mining rights on a continental shelf and rights on the superadjacent waters necessary to protect those submarine rights. See Restatement (Third), § 511. Under the proposed Law of the Sea Treaty, states may claim a territorial sea of up to 12 miles and an Exclusive Economic Zone (EEZ) of no more than 200 miles. (For a discussion of the law of the sea, see Sohn, The Law of the Sea in a Nutshell (1984).)

c. *Airspace.* Each state has exclusive jurisdiction over the air space above its land territory and territorial waters. Therefore, authorized use of that airspace by either civil or military aircraft of another state can occur only by the express agreement of the subjacent nation. See e.g., Chicago Convention on International Civil Aviation (1944).

Originally, it was assumed that jurisdiction extended upward without limit. With the advent of space flight it became clear that there were limits to the jurisdiction of states over airspace. Although there are no conventional definitions of the precise outer limits of national jurisdiction in airspace, it appears that there is general acceptance of a principle that there is an upper boundary marking the beginning of an area of "free use" of outer space, analogous to the doctrine of freedom of the seas.

§ **7–6. The protective principle.** This principle permits a state to exercise jurisdiction over conduct outside its territory that threatens its security, as long as that conduct is generally recognized as criminal by states in the international community. Restatement (Third), § 402(3). Under it, a state's jurisdiction is determined with reference to the national interest threatened by the foreign act. The principle is, in this way, directly related to, but distinguishable from, the objective territoriality principle. While the latter permits a state to protect primarily *private* interests against *actual* injury, the former recognizes a state's interest in protecting governmental interests against the *threat* of harm. One danger inherent in broad assertions of the principle lies in its possible use to punish acts committed abroad that are specifically protected as civil liberties by the state within whose territory they occur, e.g. freedom of speech or press.

§ **7–7. The universality principle.** The "universality" principle recognizes that certain activities, universally dangerous to states and their subjects, require authority in all community members to punish such acts wherever they may occur, even absent a link between the state and the parties or the acts in question. Universal jurisdiction has traditionally been asserted over the crime of piracy on the high seas because any nation that apprehended and punished a pirate acted in the community interest. After World War II, strong arguments were advanced, based largely on the principles of the Nuremberg Trials and various United Nations resolutions, that perpetrators of genocide and crimes against humanity were also subject to universal jurisdiction. The Israeli Government justified the trial (but not the kidnapping) of Adolf Eichmann in part, under the universality principle. In addition, aircraft piracy, engaging in the slave trade and some forms of terrorism, especially terrorism aimed at diplomats, may be subject to universal jurisdiction. § 404, Restatement (Third).

A group of international agreements including the Hague Convention for the Suppression of Unlawful Seizure of Aircraft, the Montreal Convention for the Suppression of Unlawful Acts against the Safety of Civil Aviation, the Convention on the Prevention and Punishment of Crimes against Internationally Protected Persons, Including Diplomatic Agents, and the International Convention on the Suppression and Punishment of the Crime of Apartheid may suggest customary legal recognition that the crimes described in them are subject to universal jurisdiction. Some of these agreements provide that parties are obligated to punish violators, even though such offenses are not committed within the party's territory or by its nationals.

§ 7–8. The passive personality principle. Under this principle a state claims jurisdiction over acts committed abroad solely because they injure a national of the claiming state. This principle is related to the universality principle in that it is invoked only where the state claiming jurisdiction has no other connection with the act. Historically, the English speaking counties and France have rejected this principle; some other states have adopted it. A majority of the Permanent Court of International Justice refused to rule on arguments embodying the principle in The Lotus Case. Although the protective principle is not generally accepted as a valid jurisdictional principle of customary international law, it has found some recent revival in connection with cases involving terrorism or other intentional injury to a state's nationals for political purposes. See § 402, Reporter's Note 3, Restatement (Third).

III. JURISDICTIONAL PRINCIPLES IN UNITED STATES LAW

§ 7–9. The role of international law. In the United States the Supremacy Clause of the Constitution, Article VI, makes federal legislation binding upon the courts. Thus, United States courts must obey any clear congressional mandate, even if to do so will place the United States in violation of international customary law restricting jurisdiction. United States v. Aluminum Co. of America, 148 F.2d 416, 443 (2d Cir.1945) (hereinafter Alcoa);

The Over the Top, 5 F.2d 838 (D.C.Conn.1925). Where legislative intent about the territorial reach of the law is unclear, courts will assume that the legislature did not intend to require a violation of international jurisdictional principles. The Charming Betsy, 6 U.S. (2 Cranch) 64, 118 (1804). They therefore use the customary jurisdictional principles described above to determine the legislation's permissible territorial scope. In addition, courts use principles of international comity to resolve actual or potential conflicts of jurisdiction once it is clear that the links between the United States and the regulated person or activity are sufficiently strong to meet a minimal international standard for jurisdiction.

§ 7–10. The "conduct" and "effects" tests in U.S. law. The "pure" territoriality theory supports the application of United States law to conduct that occurs in United States territory. § 402, Restatement (Third). As long as the conduct occurring within the United States is prohibited, the effects of that conduct need not be felt in the United States in order for United States law to govern. Generally, the conduct must be the conduct prohibited by the law sought to be applied, not merely conduct conceptually related to it. United States v. Columba-Colella, 604 F.2d 356 (5th Cir. 1979).

The "effects test" became part of United States federal law in *Alcoa,* supra at 443, when the court adopted the objective territoriality theory of the

S.S. Lotus Case, supra. Judge Learned Hand, sitting for the U.S. Supreme Court that could not muster a disinterested quorum, ruled that the Sherman Act applied to a foreign agreement that was intended to affect U.S. trade and did so, even though that agreement was solely between foreign companies and was performed entirely on foreign soil. Cf. § 415, Restatement (Third).

Some courts argue that in antitrust cases the effect must be "substantial", to meet international requirements, Timberlane Lumber Co. v. Bank of America N.T. & S.A., 549 F.2d 597, 608–15 (9th Cir. 1976). Since Judge Hand, in *Alcoa,* ruled that an effect on U.S. trade would be presumed, absent a contrary showing, if an *intent* to effect U.S. trade was demonstrated, some commentators have argued that an intent to effect U.S. trade is alone enough to establish jurisdiction to prescribe. In cases involving antifraud provisions of the securities law, the fact that securities of U.S. companies are involved or that the securities are traded on a U.S. securities exchange will subject foreign sellers acting abroad to Reg. 10(b)(5) under the Securities and Exchange Act of 1934. Bersch v. Drexel Firestone, 519 F.2d 974 (2d Cir.1975), cert. denied, 423 U.S. 1018 (1975). Some cases suggest that the required effect need not be as substantial to support a private cause of action for securities fraud as would be required to apply the U.S. registration requirements. Compare Continental Grain (Australia) Pty. Ltd. v. Pacific Oilseeds, Inc., 592 F.2d

409 (8th Cir.1979), with Report on Proposed SEC Rules, 21 Rec.N.Y.C.Bar Ass'n 240 (1966).

§ 7–11. **The protective principle in U.S. law.** The protective principle has had limited use in United States domestic adjudication, perhaps because of the common law's preference for jurisdiction tied to territorial relationships. United States courts have invoked the protective principle, for example, to punish perjury before a U.S. consular officer, Rocha v. United States, 288 F.2d 545 (9th Cir.1961); United States v. Pizzarusso, 388 F.2d 8 (2d Cir.1968); and to punish a foreign conspiracy to smuggle heroin into the United States, Rivard v. United States, 375 F.2d 882 (5th Cir.1967).

§ 7–12. **Comity in U.S. law.** Where both the United States and another country or countries have sufficient contacts to permit the exercise of jurisdiction under international legal principles, United States courts have developed a doctrine of judicial restraint based on the principle of comity to resolve international jurisdictional conflicts. The practical necessity of arriving at a principled method for such accommodation was stated by Justice Jackson in Lauritzen v. Larsen, 345 U.S. 571 (1953), where he articulated the distinction between the existence of national power and the wisdom of its exercise.

  [International law] aims at stability and order through usages which considerations of comity, reciprocity and long-range interest have developed to define the domain which each nation will claim as its own. . . . [i]n dealing with international commerce we cannot be unmindful of the necessity for mutual forbearance if retaliations are to be avoided; nor should we forget that any contact which we hold sufficient to warrant application of our law to a foreign transaction will logically be as strong a warrant for a foreign country to apply its law to an American transaction. Id. at 582.

The comity principle is most accurately characterized as a golden rule among nations—that each must give the respect to the laws, policies and interests of others that it would have others give to its own in the same or similar circumstances. This principle informs decisions whose goal is to reconcile the fact of national territorial authority with an international system in which persons and goods must move across national borders. Maier, "Resolving Extraterritorial Conflicts or 'There and Back Again'," 25 Va.J.Int.L. 7, 13–16 (1984). As one court has put it

Comity is a recognition which one nation extends within its own territory to the legislative, executive, or judicial acts of another. It is not a rule of law, but one of practice, convenience, and expediency. . . . [i]t is a nation's expression of understanding which demonstrates due regard both to international duty and convenience and to the rights of persons protected by its own laws. Somportex Ltd. v. Philadelphia Chewing

Gum Corp., 453 F.2d 435, 440 (3d Cir.1971), cert. denied, 405 U.S. 1017 (1972).

In the United States, courts have resorted to the comity principle both as a rationale for refusing to apply United States law to foreign persons or events in situations where concurrent jurisdiction exists, and for refusing to give effect to a foreign nation's law, if that nation has breached its duty of comity to the United States. Hilton v. Guyot, 159 U.S. 113 (1895).

Section 40, of the Restatement (Second) identified several factors to be weighed to determine whether jurisdiction, otherwise existing under international legal principles, should be exercised. Those factors included the vital national interests of each of the states, the extent and nature of the hardship that inconsistent commands would impose on the parties subject to conflicting national decisions, the extent to which any required conduct would have to take place within the territory of another state, the nationality of the persons subject to concurrent jurisdiction and the extent to which enforcement by either state could be expected to achieve compliance with that state's rule.

During the mid-1970's, courts in the United States developed a jurisprudence of interest balancing, based on the elements of § 40, Restatement (Second), plus additional factors, to determine when existing United States jurisdiction should nonetheless not be exercised. See Timberlane Lumber Co. v. Bank of America, N.T. & S.A., 549

F.2d 597 (9th Cir.1976); Manningtom Mills v. Congoleum Corp., 595 F.2d 1287 (3d Cir.1979).

Section 403 of the Restatement (Third) adopts the interest-balancing principle and concludes that customary international law prohibits exercising jurisdiction over any events or persons when such exercise is unreasonable in the light of the relative interests of the states involved. Later sections represent specific applications of the earlier principles with respect to taxation (§§ 411–413), extraterritorial control over foreign subsidiaries of U.S. corporations (§ 414), antitrust (§ 415), securities (§ 416), foreign sovereign compulsion (§ 441), and production of foreign situs documents (§ 442). §§ 431–433 deal with jurisdiction to enforce and §§ 421–423 with jurisdiction to adjudicate.

In Laker Airways, Ltd. v. Sabena, Belgian World Airways, 731 F.2d 909 (D.C.Cir.1984), the District of Columbia Circuit rejected the proposition that international law required interest balancing with exclusive jurisdiction in the state having the greatest interest. Rather, each state having the minimal link with a transaction or person could exercise jurisdiction under international law, any conflicts to be resolved through diplomatic channels. This conclusion is reflected in the Restatement (Third) which provides that when two or more states seek to exercise conflicting concurrent jurisdiction each state has an obligation to evaluate its own as well as the other state's interest in exercising jurisdiction, in the light of all relevant factors . . .; a state should defer to the other state if that state's interest is clearly greater. Sec. 403(3).

This section suggests that such conflicts are to be resolved by means of consultation and negotiation, not by resort to an overriding legal rule, § 403, comment e, and thus reflects the principle of comity embodied in the earlier § 40, Restatement (Second). See Maier, "Interest Balancing and Extraterritorial Jurisdiction," 31 Am.J.Comp.L. 579 (1983).

§ **7–13. Comity and reciprocity.** The use of the comity principle above should be sharply distinguished from its use as a device to involve the courts in the international political process by using lack of reciprocal treatment abroad as a reason for refusing otherwise fair treatment to foreigners in a U.S. forum. In Hilton v. Guyot, supra, the United States refused to enforce a French judgment on the grounds that in a similar situation France would not give effect to a United States judgment. The Court wrote:

> . . . [i]nternational law is founded upon mutuality and reciprocity, and—by the principles of international law recognized in most civilized nations, and by the comity of our own country the judgment is not entitled to be considered conclusive. Id. at 228.

The French judgment was refused enforcement, not because it was in error, but to convince the

French court that in later cases it should decide in favor of United States judgments.

This decision, by requiring reciprocity as a prerequisite to the grant of comity by United States courts, treated the comity doctrine as a political principle to be applied to advance United States policies, not as a doctrine useful to reflect international community interests in developing and preserving an effective international legal system. The reciprocity requirement for the enforcement of foreign judgments in *Hilton* is generally disfavored today. § 98, Restatement (Second) of Conflict of Laws (1971).

§ 7–14. **Sovereign Compulsion.** The sovereign compulsion defense is a rule of municipal law under which a court or other agency will not require compliance with otherwise applicable forum law in the face of a contrary command by a foreign sovereign acting properly within its own jurisdiction. The defense is most often encountered in cases involving the production of documentary evidence located abroad. The defense is often paired for discussion with the act of state doctrine and is sometimes confused with it. Unlike the act of state doctrine or the principle of sovereign immunity, the sovereign compulsion defense does not stem from considerations of international comity or separation of powers but rather is designed to avoid unfairness to a private party who faces actual or potential contradictory commands from his own and another sovereign. It is not a jurisdictional principle but rather a rule about how the forum will treat conflicting commands based on valid concurrent jurisdiction. The sovereign compulsion defense is, thus, more appropriately viewed as a rule of private, rather than public, international law, because it is a doctrine of forum restraint derived from principles of fairness designed to protect private parties. It embodies principles of fairness and reflects the need to coordinate the exercise of national jurisdiction in the interest of an effectively operating international system. Société Internationale Pour Participations Industrielles et Commerciales, S.A. v. Rogers, 357 U.S. 197 (1958).

In Interamerican Refining Corp. v. Texas Maracaibo, Inc., 307 F.Supp. 1291 (D.Del.1970), a private treble-damage action under the antitrust laws, Venezuelan subsidiaries of defendant American companies had refused to sell oil to plaintiff. Admitting the refusal, defendant argued that the Venezuelan government had ordered him to refuse to deal. The court wrote:

> When a nation compels a trade practice, firms there have no choice but to obey. Acts of business become effectively acts of the sovereign . . . Anticompetitive practices compelled by foreign nations are not restraints of commerce . . . because refusal to comply would put an end to commerce. Id. at 1298.

The Court said that the sovereign compulsion defense was applicable since the defendant had not solicited the Venezuelan government's boycott. Id. at 1297. See Occidental Petroleum Corp. v. Buttes Gas & Oil Co., 331 F.Supp. 92, 107–8 (C.D.Cal.1971).

The sovereign compulsion defense has been asserted with varying degrees of success in numerous cases in which production of foreign-based documents by parties before the forum court would violate the law of the documents' situs. See, e.g., Société Internationale v. Rogers, supra; In re Application of Chase Manhattan Bank, 297 F.2d 611 (2d Cir.1962); United States v. Field, 532 F.2d 404 (5th Cir.1976); Ohio v. Arthur Andersen & Co., 570 F.2d 1370 (10th Cir.1978); In re Westinghouse Electric Corp. Uranium Contracts Litigation, 563 F.2d 992 (10th Cir.1977); United States v. Bank of Nova Scotia, 691 F.2d 1384 (11th Cir.1982); United States v. First National Bank of Chicago, 699 F.2d 341 (7th Cir.1983); Marc Rich & Co. v. United States, 707 F.2d 663 (2d Cir.1983). Normally, the party ordered to produce the documents will not be punished for contempt for failing to do so if a good faith effort to procure them has been made and if foreign criminal penalties will be assessed if they are produced in response to the U.S. court order. 357 U.S. at 211. The Convention on the Taking of Evidence Abroad in Civil or Commercial Matters represents an effort to resolve some of these conflicts by international agreement. The U.S. Supreme Court has ruled that under this Convention comity requires the courts to mitigate the exercise of enforcement authority to protect foreign litigants against unduly burdensome or unnecessary judicial discovery orders. Societe Nationale Industrielle Aerospatiale, et al. v. United States Dist. Ct. for the Southern Dist. of Iowa, 482 U.S. 522 (1987).

CHAPTER 8

FOREIGN RELATIONS LAW IN THE UNITED STATES

I. INTRODUCTION

Most of the foreign relations law in the United States deals with the divisions of power between branches of the federal government or between the federal government and the states in matters touching foreign affairs. These issues are always determined under federal law. This chapter provides an overview of the most important of these power allocations. It includes a discussion of federal preemption of state power in these matters and a consideration of some of the separation of powers issues that arise between the federal branches in the foreign affairs field. Principal emphasis is given to those issues involving the quantum and scope of executive power in this area. Included are the treaty power, the recognition power and the war powers. The chapter concludes with a discussion of the role of customary international law in the law of the United States.

II. THE ROLE OF THE STATES

§ 8–1. **Federal supremacy.** There is some authority for the proposition that the location of the foreign affairs power in the federal government,

186

rather than in the states, is a necessary attribute of sovereignty itself and, therefore, needs no constitutional source other than the intent to create a nation. United States v. Curtiss-Wright Export Corp., 299 U.S. 304 (1936). In fact, constitutional history makes it clear that matters touching foreign affairs were intended to be dealt with under national law. See, e.g., The Federalist, Nos. 1–6, 8–9, 11, 21, 49. First, all the important foreign affairs powers are explicitly denied to the states. They may not, without the consent of Congress, enter into international agreements, assess charges against imports or exports, keep military forces or engage in war. They are absolutely prohibited from entering separate alliances. U.S. Const., art. I, § 10. In many instances, the U.S. Constitution explicitly assigns law-making power to the national government e.g., the power to regulate foreign commerce or immigration. The supremacy clause, U.S. Const., art. VI, makes both legislation passed pursuant to such provisions and international agreements binding upon the states as the law of the land. States may not directly contravene such federal law, even in areas in which, absent such national action, they would have authority to legislate. Ware v. Hylton, 3 U.S. (3 Dall.) 199, 296–97 (1796); Missouri v. Holland, 252 U.S. 416 (1920). When such overlapping authority exists, state courts have balanced the importance of state authority against the need for national control. Such cases have included matters relating to decedents' estates, In re Estate of Kish, 52 N.J. 454, 246 A.2d

1 (1968); state human rights laws, N.Y. Times Co. v. City of New York Comm. on Human Rights, 41 N.Y.2d 345, 393 N.Y.S. 312, 361 N.E.2d 963 (1977); requirements that state governments buy American made goods, K.S.B. Technical Sales Corp. v. North Jersey Dist. Water Supply Comm., 75 N.J. 272, 381 A.2d 774 (1977); and state prohibitions on dealing with or investing in the Republic of South Africa, Springfield Rare Coin Galleries v. Johnson, 115 Ill.2d 221, 104 Ill.Dec. 743, 503 N.E.2d 300 (1986). Even where there is no direct conflict between state and federal law, the national government may be found to have "occupied the field" to such an extent that states may not legislate in the interstices of the federal legislation. See, e.g., Hines v. Davidowitz, 312 U.S. 52 (1941); Cf. De-Canas v. Bica, 424 U.S. 351 (1976).

In some instances, the very nature of certain subject matter may preclude state action, Zschernig v. Miller, 389 U.S. 429, 443 (1968) (Stewart, J., concurring), and state interference with specific federal policies, not reduced to legislative form, is prohibited. See United States v. Belmont, 301 U.S. 324 (1937). States may not act to exacerbate relations with foreign nations, Banco Nacional de Cuba v. Sabbatino, 376 U.S. 398, 423 (1964), nor may they contravene the policies advanced in a U.S. international agreement even if no direct conflict with the agreement exists. Kolovrat v. Oregon, 366 U.S. 187 (1961). In those situations where no direct preemption of state law occurs, the cases indicate that whether a particular decision is appropriate for the national rather than the state governments can be determined by examining three factors:

(1) whether the limited constituency of the state provides an appropriate political context in which to make the required policy judgment;

(2) whether the pertinent information which must be weighed to determine the wisdom of the policy decision is available to the state decision-maker, and

(3) whether any potential adverse effects of the decision will fall upon the entire nation or will be localized within the particular state. Maier, "The Bases and Range of Federal Common Law in Private International Matters," 5 Vand.J.Trans.L. 133, 168 (1971).

III.   SEPARATION OF POWERS IN FOREIGN AFFAIRS

§ 8–2. **Executive power.** Although Article I of the Constitution specifically allocates legislative power over some foreign affairs matters to the Congress, most of the authority in international affairs lies in the executive branch. Article II allocates few specific foreign affairs powers to the executive. The President is expressly given authority to receive and appoint ambassadors and the power to make treaties, with the consent of two thirds of the Senate art. II, §§ 2 & 3. All other presidential powers in foreign affairs are derived from the express grant of executive power in the first sentence of article II. Thus, the fullness of executive power results from a kind of implicit "necessary and proper" clause, read into this grant of authority. Much of the content for this general executive power is derived from customary practice, often as the result of intragovernmental contention between the executive and legislative branches for the right to exercise a given element of foreign affairs authority.

The dynamics of this constitutional law-formation process are described in Youngstown Sheet and Tube Co. v. Sawyer (Steel Seizure), 343 U.S. 579 (1952). When the U.S. steel industry could not avoid a strike, President Truman issued an executive order, without express statutory authority, directing the Secretary of Commerce to seize and operate the steel mills. The President explicitly tied this action to the need for steel in the war effort. The U.S. Supreme Court affirmed an injunction against the President's order on the grounds that it was unconstitutional, in part because it was not authorized by Congress and, perhaps, implicitly prohibited by the Taft Hartley Act.

Rejecting judicial definitions of "the art of governing under our Constitution," Justice Jackson, concurring, wrote:

   1. When the President acts pursuant to an express or implied authorization of Congress, his authority is at its maximum, for it includes all that he possesses in his own right plus all that

Congress can delegate. . . . If his act is held unconstitutional under these circumstances, it usually means that the Federal Government as an undivided whole lacks power.

2.   When the President acts in absence of either a congressional grant or denial of authority, he can only rely upon his own independent powers, but there is a zone of twilight in which he and Congress may have concurrent authority, or in which its distribution is uncertain. . . . In this area, any actual test of power is likely to depend on the imperatives of events and contemporary imponderables rather than on abstract theories of law.

3.   When the President takes measures incompatible with the expressed or implied will of Congress, his power is at its lowest ebb, for then he can rely only upon his own constitutional powers minus any constitutional powers of Congress over the matter. Courts can sustain exclusive Presidential control in such a case only by disabling the Congress from acting upon the subject. Id. at 635–638.

In Dames and Moore v. Reagan, 453 U.S. 654 (1981), the Court adopted a modified version of Jackson's analysis in a case that did not fit precisely within any of the three *Steel Seizure* categories. In that case, creditors of the Iranian government sought a declaration that the executive action, nullifying their claims as part of the agreement for the release of a group of American citizens held hostage by Iran's revolutionary government, was unconstitutional. Id. at 662–68. Relying heavily on the *Steel Seizure Case,* supra, the Court concluded that the Executive's action was valid. Id. at 654. The Court noted the long-standing practice of settling international claims pursuant to Presidential authority.

Unable to find specific legislative authorization for the executive act, the Court held that the general tenor of the International Emergency Economic Powers Act, 50 U.S.C. § 1701 et seq., amounted to an implicit approval of the practice of claim settlement by executive agreement. The Court, in effect, recognized the existence of a continuum of legislative and executive interaction consisting of gradations between express legislative authorization and inherent executive power, a more flexible concept than Jackson's discrete categories. It is clear from these cases that guides to the scope of executive power in foreign affairs are not found primarily in judicial definitions or even in the synthesis of results in decided cases. Rather that authority is defined in an interbranch demand-response-accommodation process similar to that which creates customary international law among nations. See Maier, Testimony on "Emergency Controls on International Economic Transactions," Hearings on proposed repeal of Sec. 5(b), Trading with the Enemy Act, Subcomm. on International Economic Policy and Trade, Comm. on

For.Rel., U.S. House of Rep., 95th Cong., 1st Sess. (Mar. 29, 1977), pp. 20–32; 44–51.

§ 8–3. The Political Question Doctrine. The general hesitancy of courts to resolve controversies between the political branches is reflected in the "political question doctrine." That hesitancy grows in large part from a fear that judicial definitions of constitutional power may inhibit the smooth functioning of governmental system in the future. Judicial characterizations run too great a risk of crystallizing erroneous judicial perceptions of appropriate power allocations that are better informed by the political and practical exigencies of everyday executive and legislative decision-making, not by abstract principles applied in the rarified atmosphere of detached constitutional analysis.

The modern statement of the political question doctrine is found in Baker v. Carr, 369 U.S. 186 (1962). In that non-foreign affairs case involving the apportionment of state legislative districts, the Court pointed out that the doctrine did not necessarily bar judicial determination solely because a case touched foreign relations. It identified six factors to be used to determine when a political question was raised. They were

a textually demonstrable constitutional commitment of the issue to a coordinate political department; or a lack of judicially discoverable and manageable standards for resolving it; or the impossibility of deciding without an initial policy determination of a kind clearly for non-judicial discretion; or the impossibility of a court's undertaking independent resolution without expressing lack of the respect due coordinate branches of the government; or an unusual need for unquestioning adherence to a political decision already made; or the potentiality of embarrassment from multifarious pronouncements by various departments on one question. Id. at 217.

Under the *Baker* test, the courts will not only avoid using their authority to interfere with the performance of the political functions assigned to the other branches, but will define their role in the light of the functional parameters of the judicial power assigned to them under article III. Thus, in Goldwater v. Carter, 444 U.S. 996 (1979), Justice Powell, concurring, summarized the *Baker* factors in terms of three inquiries:

(i) Does the issue involve resolution of questions committed by the text of the Constitution to a coordinate branch of government? (ii) Would resolution of the question demand that a court move beyond areas of judicial expertise? (iii) Do prudential considerations counsel against judicial intervention? Id. at 998.

Application of these principles is illustrated in Ramirez v. Weinberger, 745 F.2d 1500 (D.C.Cir. 1984), remanded for reconsideration on other grounds, 105 S.Ct. 2353 (1985). In that case, a U.S. citizen challenged the authority of the executive branch effectively to confiscate his plantation in

Honduras by permitting its use for military exercises to train soldiers for El Salvador. The Court concluded that the claims were not "exclusively committed for resolution to the political branches" for three reasons: federal courts historically have resolved disputes over land, adjudication of this claim was not beyond judicial expertise and none of the circumstances of the case gave rise to prudential concerns. Id. at 1512–13.

§ 8–4. **Recognition.** When an extraordinary political event occurs—the emergence of a new state or the rise to power of a new government by other than routine processes—other nations in the world community indicate their willingness to accept both the fact of change and the legal consequences arising from that fact by recognizing the new state or government. Although some authorities see recognition as a condition precedent to legal "existance" in the international community (the constitutive theory), the better view is that recognition is a declaratory act, indicating the willingness of the recognizing government to treat with the new entity or government under the existing international legal regime.

It is important to distinguish recognition of a foreign government from recognition of a new state and from the question of maintaining diplomatic relations. Legal rights and obligations accrue to states, not governments. Therefore, recognizing a state is a statement that the entity in question will be treated by the recognizer as having legal rights and duties under the international system. Criteria for recognizing a state include whether it has effective control over a defined territory and population, an organized governmental administration, and the capacity to act effectively to conduct foreign relations and to fulfill international obligations. Dept. of State.Bull. File L/AF, reprinted in Rovine, Digest of United States Practice in International Law 17 (1973). International law does not *require* recognition of a state, even when these conditions are met. G. von Glahn, "Law Among Nations," 90 (1981); J. Crawford, "The Creation of States in International Law," 12 (1979).

The government is a spokesman for the state's people and recognizing it merely signifies that it will be treated as having the sole right to assert the country's claims and responses and to participate in arriving at accommodations with other states. Recognizing a new state does not necessarily include recognition of its government but normally does so. Whether to recognize a government is solely a matter of domestic policy, not of international law. H. Kelsen, Principles of International Law, 400 (1966).

Establishing diplomatic relations with a new government is not required as a part of the recognition process, although they usually go hand in hand. Breaking diplomatic relations merely signifies that one state declines to deal with another's government, but does not vitiate the recognition of that government. A government loses recognition only when a new one is recognized in its place. Severing diplomatic relations implies overt hostility while failure to recognize generally has a neutral implication.

In the United States, the power to recognize foreign governments is inferred from the express grant of the power to "receive Ambassadors and other public Ministers" in art. II, § 3, of the Constitution. L. Henkin, Foreign Affairs and the Constitution, 178 (1972). Whether a government should be recognized is a political question whose determination is within the exclusive prerogative of the executive branch. Banco Nacional de Cuba v. Sabbatino, 376 U.S. 398, 410 (1964); National City Bank of New York v. Republic of China, 348 U.S. 356, 358 (1955); Guaranty Trust Co. v. United States, 304 U.S. 126, 137–8 (1938). The President also has power to enter into agreements that are necessary to recognition. United States v. Pink, 315 U.S. 203, 230 (1942). When he does so, conditions necessary to recognition will supercede state law, even though they are not reflected in a formal treaty. When President Roosevelt recognized the Soviet Government in 1933, he also accepted an assignment (the "Litvinov Assignment") of all rights in United States-situs property claimed by the Soviets under expropriation decrees issued after the Russian Revolution. State courts refused to recognize that the Soviets had acquired any rights to assign because state law denied extraterritorial effect to such takings. The U.S. Supreme

Court held that accepting the Assignment was an essential condition to recognition to normalize relations between the United States and the Soviet Union. Therefore, U.S. rights under it could not be questioned under state law. United States v. Belmont, 301 U.S. 324, 330 (1937).

Recognition has been used as a political tool by the United States government in the past, but current policy is to recognize governments that in fact have established control over the state. 2 M. Whiteman, Digest of International Law, 69 (1963). Recognition today is deemed not to imply approval of a new government but only willingness to communicate. See generally, L.T. Galloway, Recognizing Foreign Governments, 30–103 (1978). Rights of recognized governments in the United States include the right to claim sovereign immunity to the same extent as other recognized governments, access to the country's U.S. bank deposits and other property, the right to receive diplomatic protection and to bring a law suit in courts in the U.S. On the other hand, a non-recognized government may be sued in its private capacity with no reciprocal rights to sue. Upright v. Mercury Business Machines, 13 A.D.2d 36, 38–41, 213 N.Y.S.2d 417, 419–22 (1961). Courts will not deny a *bona fide* recognized government the rights that it would normally have under United States law solely because diplomatic relations with it have been broken. Banco Nacional de Cuba v. Sabbatino, 376 U.S. 398, 410 (1964).

Goldwater v. Carter, 444 U.S. 996 (1979), the most recent U.S. Supreme Court decision on the question, raises questions about the current scope of judicial review in recognition cases. In that case, a group of U.S. Senators sued to prevent President Carter from recognizing the government of the People's Republic of China and withdrawing recognition from the government of Taiwan. The District of Columbia Circuit found that the case presented a justiciable question but that the executive branch had not exceeded its authority. Goldwater v. Carter, 617 F.2d 697, 709 (D.C.Cir.1979).

The Supreme Court remanded the case with directions to dismiss the complaint. Goldwater v. Carter, 444 U.S. 996 (1979). Four separate opinions were filed. Justice Powell found that the issue was not yet ripe for adjudication but would be so if the President and the Congress reached an impass. Id. at 997–1002. Justice Rehnquist, with Burger, Stewart and Stevens, voted to dismiss on political question grounds. Id. at 1002–06. Justices Blackmun and White voted to hear the case. Id. at 1006. Justice Brennan believed that the case involved solely constitutional interpretation to determine which branch held the power to terminate a treaty. He concluded that the President had the power incident to his recognition of the People's Republic of China. Id. at 1006–07.

§ 8–5. The international agreement power. The power to make international agreements is lodged in the executive branch, giving the president a powerful tool for the conduct of foreign relations. International agreements fall into two broad categories: treaties and executive agreements. See generally, Weinberger v. Rossi, 456 U.S. 25 (1982). The term treaty is a technical characterization applied to those international agreements made by the President with the advice and consent of two-thirds of the Senate, U.S. Const., art. II, § 2. Executive agreements are made by the President pursuant to authority granted in legislation or in a prior treaty or acting alone under his sole constitutional authority founded in the power to receive ambassadors, United States v. Belmont, supra, the commander-in-chief power, See "Acquisition of Naval and Air Bases in Exchange for Over-Age Destroyers," 39 Op.A.G. 484 (1940), and the authority to "take care that the laws be faithfully executed," U.S. Const., art. II, § 3. See also Dames & Moore v. Regan, 453 U.S. 654 (1981).

The authority of the United States to enter into international agreements is coextensive with the foreign affairs interests of the United States. The scope of this power is determined by U.S. law, not by international law.

The treaty power, as expressed in the Constitution, is in terms unlimited except by those restraints which are found in that instrument against the action of the government itself and of that of the States. It would not be contended that it extends so far as to authorize what the

Constitution forbids, or a change in the character of the government or in that of one of the
States, or a cession of any portion of the territory
without its consent. . . . But with these exceptions, it is not perceived that there is any limit to
the question which can be adjusted touching any
matter which is properly the subject of negotiations with a foreign country.

Geofroy v. Riggs, 133 U.S. 258, 267 (1890); See
Santovincenzo v. Egan, 284 U.S. 30, 40 (1931).

It has been suggested that the international
agreement power extends only to matters generally recognized as being connected to foreign relations. See Hughes, 1929 Proceedings, Am. Soc'y
Int'l L. 196; Cf. Power Authority of New York v.
Federal Power Commission, 247 F.2d 538 (D.C.Cir.
1957), vacated, 355 U.S. 64 (1957). It is now, however, conceded that the United States may enter
into an international agreement on any matter
that is of mutual interest to it and a foreign
nation. The international agreement power is not
limited by any powers reserved to the states. Ibid.;
Ware v. Hylton, 3 U.S. (3 Dall.) 199, 236–37 (1796);
see Missouri v. Holland, 252 U.S. 416, 433–35
(1920). A treaty is, of course, subject to Constitutional limitations on governmental power and may
not contravene specific constitutional prohibitions.
Reid v. Covert, 354 U.S. 1 (1957). See generally,
Restatement (Third) § 302.

Treaties and international executive agreements
may be either self-executing or non-self-executing.

A self-executing agreement becomes internal law in the United States immediately upon entry into force internationally. This means that courts will look to it for the rule of decision in cases affected by its terms. Non-self-executing agreements require legislation to implement them domestically. For such agreements it is the implementing legislation, not the agreement itself, that becomes the rule of decision in U.S. courts.

Although it is clear today that both treaties and executive agreements are constitutionally acceptable instruments for conducting U.S foreign policy, there are some differences between the two types of agreements in terms of their domestic legal effect. Under U.S. law, a self-executing treaty has a normative rank equal to that of a federal statute. See U.S. Constitution, art. VI; Restatement (third) § 111. As such, it supersedes all prior federal statutes in conflict with it and all state laws whether prior or later in time. See, e.g., U.S. v. Palestine Liberation Organization, 695 F.Supp. 1456 (S.D.N.Y.1988); Asakura v. Seattle, 265 U.S. 332 (1924). The normative rank of self-executing executive agreements depends upon their character. That is to say, executive agreements authorized by a federal statute or treaty have the same normative rank as the statute or treaty on which they are based, with the later in time having precedence. Presidential executive agreements, viz., agreements made by the President in the exercise of his constitutional power, will supersede inconsistent state laws but may not prevail against a conflicting prior federal statute. See Belmont v. U.S., 301 U.S. 324 (1937); U.S. v. Pink, 315 U.S. 203 (1942); U.S. v. Guy W. Capps, Inc., 204 F.2d 655 (4th Cir.1953), aff'd on other grounds, 348 U.S. 296 (1955). See also, Dames & Moore v. Regan, supra. Whether the latter proposition is always true or applies only when the President exercises powers that he shares with the Congress remains to be settled by the courts. See Restatement (Third) § 115, Reporters' Notes 5. But whether an executive agreement supersedes prior federal legislation should depend upon the character of the agreement and not upon the erroneous assumption that executive agreements in general have a second class status. See, e.g., South Puerto Rico Sugar Co. Trading Corp. v. U.S., 167 Ct.Cl. 236, 334 F.2d 622 (1964).

A finding that a treaty is either self-executing or non-self-executing has no effect on the international obligation of the United States to carry out the treaty. Until a non-self-executing treaty is executed, however, the U.S. may be effectively disabled from carrying out its obligations under the treaty because it has not exercised the authority to do whatever internal acts are necessary in order to meet that obligation. Courts in the United States say that whether an agreement is self-executing is determined by the intent of the states parties as indicated by the language in the treaty. Foster v. Neilson, 27 U.S. (2 Pet.) 253, 314 (1829). In fact, whether a treaty will be treated as being self-executing is a decision based on domestic policy. Therefore, if the treaty deals with subject-matter over which Congress has sole competence to legislate, such as appropriation of money, or its execution without implementing legislation appears to be difficult or impracticable, the courts will normally find the treaty to be non-self-executing, regardless of the apparent intent of the parties. See Stein, "When is an International Agreement Self-Executing in American Law?", Report for the Sixth International Congress of Comparative Law, 1962; Yuji Iwasawa, "The Doctrine of Self–Executive Treaties in the United States: A Critical Analysis," 26 Va.J.Int'l L. 627 (1986).

The nature and role of a self-executing treaty was considered most recently in Edwards v. Carter, 580 F.2d 1055 (D.C.Cir.1978). In that case some members of the House sought to prevent the transfer of the Panama Canal under the Panama Canal Treaty on the grounds that the House had to approve all transfers of U.S. property. The Court of Appeals affirmed the district court's dismissal of the case, saying that the Constitution did not grant exclusive competence to the House to effect property transfers and that therefore transfers could be effected by other constitutional means such as a treaty. Id. at 1057–61.

Congressional concern over the use of the treaty power surfaced in the early 1950's when several constitutional amendments (known as the Bricker

Amendments) were submitted in an effort to limit the self-executing effect of both treaties and executive agreements and to define the boundaries between the treaty power and the executive agreement power. These amendments never achieved sufficient congressional approval to submit them to the states. On this subject, See Buergenthal, International Human Rights in a Nutshell 213–20 (1988). In response to these concerns, however, the Department of State adopted Circular 175, a formal document laying out the procedures to be followed, including consultative procedures, during the negotiation of any international agreement.

Circular 175 states that in determining whether a negotiated agreement will be handled as an executive agreement or a treaty, the State Department will consider the extent to which the agreement involves the nation as a whole, whether the agreement will affect state laws, whether the agreement can be self-executing, the relevant past practice concerning similar agreements, the preferences of Congress, the degree of formality of the agreement, the agreement's expected duration and general international practice in connection with the type of agreement in question.

Following disclosures of various secret executive agreements that had operated during the Vietnam War, Congress enacted the Case Act, 1 U.S.C. § 112(b). This act requires the Executive Branch to transmit the texts of all international agreements to Congress as soon as practicable after each agreement has entered into force. The shear volume of agreements transmitted has made it difficult for Congress to carry out the contemplated review function except in the case of agreements that are of special interest to particular groups of constituents.

§ 8–6. **War powers.** The President serves as Commander-in-Chief of the Armed Forces, art. II, § 2, cl. 1, and has charge of the country's foreign relations under the general grant of executive power, art. II, § 1, cl. 1. Together, these are the executive war powers. On the other hand, Congress is given the power to declare war, to raise and support armies and to provide and maintain a Navy, art. I, § 8, cls. 11–13. It also has the general power of the purse, art. I, § 7, cl. 1. These concurrent powers of the President and Congress sometimes conflict during the conduct of armed hostilities. That was the case during the Vietnam War when the executive branch continued a war in the face of significant congressional opposition but the Congress was unable to muster a majority to cut off funds for the project.

The most vituperative conflicts occur over the President's power to commit troops in situations short of war which could evolve into full scale conflicts, in effect facing the Congress with a *fait accomplis.* To deal with this situation, the Congress passed the War Powers Resolution, Nov. 7, 1973, 87 Stat. 55. The Resolution requires consultation between the President and Congress "in every possible instance" before introducing U.S. forces into hostilities or into eminent danger of hostilities. After troops are introduced in certain situations, the President is required to report to Congress concerning the circumstances. Within sixty days of such a report, the troops must be withdrawn unless Congress has authorized a continuation of the action.

The War Powers Resolution represents the first overt recognition by the Congress of the inherent power of the President to send troops abroad without prior Congressional approval. Prior to the resolution, the existence of such a power had not been confirmed by the courts who in most cases characterize these issues as political questions. See, e.g., Holtzman v. Schlesinger, 484 F.2d 1307 (2d Cir.1973); United States v. Sisson, 294 F.Supp. 511 (D.Mass.1968). Furthermore, the President can limit the effectiveness of the War Powers Resolution by consulting with Congress only after the troops are already on the way, or by equipping the troops other than with their normal combat gear, thus avoiding a triggering device of the resolution.

The Executive Branch has consistently maintained that the War Powers Resolution represents an unconstitutional congressional attempt to interfere with the powers of the President as Chief Executive and Commander in Chief. The courts are likely to treat the dispute as a political question unless an impasse should develop between the Congress and the Executive. See Goldwater v.

Carter, 444 U.S. 996, 997–1002 (Powell, J.) (1979). Lacking judicial intervention, the effect of the Resolution on executive power is determined principally by whether U.S. public opinion supports or discourages the use of U.S. troops abroad under the circumstances.

IV. CUSTOMARY INTERNATIONAL LAW IN U.S. LAW

§ 8–7. **Authority.** In Chapter I, we emphasized the importance of keeping the difference between the domestic and international applications of international law constantly in mind. We pointed out that in the United States, parties before domestic courts invoke international law whenever it appears relevant. In a very real sense, then, it is not the international legal *system* that operates in United States courts but rather those principles of international law that a U.S. court elects to apply because they are deemed to be appropriate in the particular case. In other words, it is the authority of the United States decision maker, not the authority of the community of nations, that gives legal effect to the rules of international law within the United States. See generally, Maier, "The Authoritative Sources of Customary International Law in the United States," 10 Mich.J.Int.L. 450 (1989); Cf. E. Dickenson, "The Law of Nations as Part of the Law of the United States," 116 U.Pa. L.Rev. 26 (1952).

The role of international law in U.S. law is addressed in The Paquete Habana, 175 U.S. 677 (1900). In that case, the President of the United States ordered a naval blockade of the Cuban coast "in pursuance of the laws of the United States and the law of nations applicable in such cases." Id. at 712. The blockade commander captured two fishing vessels that were sold as prize. In a suit by the original owners to recover those proceeds, the U.S. Supreme Court, sitting as a prize court, held that international law prohibited seizing coastal fishing vessels during time of war. The Court wrote:

> International law is part of our law, and must be ascertained and administered by the courts of justice of appropriate jurisdiction, as often as questions of right depending upon it are duly presented for their determination. For this purpose, where there is no treaty, and no controlling executive or legislative act or judicial decision, resort must he had to the customs and usages of civilized nations . . .. Id. at 700.

The meaning of this broad language has been the subject of considerable controversy. Some writers emphasize the first sentence in the quotation, arguing that international law is automatically and directly applicable in United States courts whenever issues to which it is relevant are up for decision. Pursuant to this analysis, customary international law is one of the "laws of the United States" that are the "supreme law of the land" under Article VI, U.S. Constitution. See e.g. L. Henkin, "International Law as Law in the United States," 82 Mich.L.Rev. 1555, 1566 (1984), and that must be "faithfully executed" by the President under Article II, Sec. 3. See J. Charney, M. Glennon, L. Henkin, "Agora: May the President Violate Customary International Law?" 80 Amer.J. Int'l L. 913 (1986). Under this view, relevant international legal rules are taken in tact for domestic use from the body of customary international law. Courts have no independent role in their interpretation or application. Henkin, supra at 1561–62.

Other writers emphasize the second sentence in the quotation, pointing out that international legal rules were relevant in *The Paquete Habana* because the President had incorporated the limitations of customary international law into his orders to the commander. Acts in violation of those rules were therefore *ultra vires* and, consequently, void. See discussion in Garcia-Mir v. Meese, 788 F.2d 1446, 1454 (11th Cir. 1986). These scholars treat customary international law as a source of principles that, like other legal principles, are applied in U.S. courts pursuant to their authority to decide cases by the common law method. See, e.g. H. Maier, "The Authoritative Sources of Customary International law in the United States," 10 Mich.J.Int'l L. 450, 473–76 (1989). Cf. Hinderlider v. La Plata River & Cherry Ditch Co., 304 U.S. 92, 110 (1938). U.S. courts normally refer to the same sources of law that are used in international forums to find the content of international law.

Their conclusions are influenced, but not compelled, by prior international judicial decisions or by the consent of the community of nations. Restatement (Third), §§ 102, 112.

In the United States, customary international law bears the same relationship to treaties that common law bears to statutory law. Thus, customary international law does not supersede pre-existing treaties in U.S. courts, even as common law rules do not supersede federal statutes.

During its work on the Restatement (Third), the American Law Institute rejected the view that a newly developed customary international legal rule could supersede a prior federal statute. Cf. Banco Nacional de Cuba v. Sabbatino, 376 U.S. 398, 423 (1964). United States courts do, however, attempt to interpret federal statutes to conform with international legal obligations, customary or conventional, Trans World Airlines, Inc. v. Franklin Mint Corp., 466 U.S. 243, 252 (1984), Weinberger v. Rossi, 456 U.S. 25, 32 (1982), unless it is clear that Congress intended a contrary result. The Charming Betsy, 6 U.S. (2 Cranch) 64, 118 (1804), United States v. Palestine Liberation Organization, 695 F.Supp. 1456, 1471 (S.D.N.Y.1988), Restatement (Third), Sections 114–15. This rule of construction is based on separation of powers considerations to prevent the judicial branch from placing the United States in violation of its international legal obligations when that result was not intended by the political branches. United States courts will give special weight to views of the executive branch in interpreting customary international law. Restatement (Third), Section 112, comment c. Customary international legal rules or principles whose existence is disputed by the United States will normally not be given effect as such by United States courts.

Customary international law is federal in nature because it implicates the foreign relations of the United States. Banco Nacional de Cuba v. Sabbatino, 376 U.S. 398, 425 (1964). Therefore, it must have a nationally uniform interpretation. Consequently, federal courts in diversity cases need not follow state court interpretions of customary international law. Jessup, "The Doctrine of Erie Railroad v. Tompkins Applied to International Law," 33 Amer.J. Int'l L. 740 (1939); Cf. Bergman v. de Sieyes, 170 F.2d 360 (2d Cir.1948).

§ 8-8. The Alien Tort Statute. A modern and important development in the role of international law in U.S. courts is found in the recent cases decided under the Alien Tort Statute, 28 U.S.C. § 1350, legislation that incorporates 'the law of nations' into U.S. law for a specific purpose. That section confers original jurisdiction on federal district courts over civil actions ". . . by an alien for a tort only, committed in violation of the law of nations or a treaty of the United States." This statute may have been designed originally to avoid international conflict by providing an objective forum in which aliens could seek redress for injuries

suffered at the hands of American citizens, either
in the U.S. or abroad, when those injuries were
such as to implicate the honor or protective duty of
the injured alien's country. Note, "The Theory of
Protective Jurisdiction," 57 N.Y.U.L.Rev. 933,
1016–17 (1982). The statute is solely a grant of
jurisdiction and does not require a particular outcome in any given case. See 26 Op.Att'y Gen. 250
(1907); Bolchos v. Darrel, 3 Fed.Cas. 810 (D.C.S.C.
1795) (No. 1607).

In Filartiga v. Pena-Irala, 630 F.2d 876 (2d Cir.
1980), the Court found jurisdiction under the Alien
Tort Statute over a claim by an alien against an
official of his own government for the torture-
slaying of plaintiff's son. Id. at 878. The Court
found that torture conducted under color of law
was a violation of the law of nations and that the
international law of human rights did not distinguish between violations directed at one's own subjects and violations directed at others. Id. at 884.
Cf. de Letelier v. Republic of Chile, 502 F.Supp. 259
(D.D.C.1980). Faced with a possible flood of cases
brought by aliens against their own governments
asserting violations of international human rights
law, the federal courts, since Filartiga, have moved
to limit that case's principles both on political
question and lack of available remedy grounds.
See e.g. Tel-Oren v. Libyan Arab Republic, 726
F.2d 774 (D.C.Cir.1984); Greenham Women
Against Cruise Missiles v. Reagan, 591 F.Supp.
1332 (S.D.N.Y.1984); Sanchez-Espinoza v. Reagan,

568 F.Supp. 596 (D.D.C.1983). The Alien Tort Statute does not grant jurisdiction in a suit against a foreign state for damages done to a private plaintiff in violation of international law. Argentine Republic v. Amerada Hess Shipping Corp., 109 S.Ct. 683, 688 (1989). Jurisdiction in such a case would lie only if the cause of action fell within one of the exceptions to immunity in Sec. 1605, Foreign Sovereign Immunities Act (FSIA).

CHAPTER 9

IMMUNITIES

I. INTRODUCTION

This chapter treats diplomatic immunity and the related areas of consular immunity and the immunity of international civil servants under both international law and the law of the United States. In addition, it discusses the principle of sovereign immunity, both as an element of federal common law and as reflected in current U.S. statutes, and the act of state doctrine as developed and applied in U.S. courts.

II. DIPLOMATIC AND RELATED IMMUNITIES

§ **9–1.** **Function.** The immunity of foreign diplomatic personnel from local actions or proceedings has long been a feature of the international legal system. Diplomatic immunity contributes to friendly relations among nations by promoting "the efficient performance of the functions of diplomatic missions as representing states . . ." Vienna Convention on Diplomatic Relations, (hereinafter cited as Convention), an essential condition for maintaining any sort of international community. In general, an accredited diplomat is immune with respect to acts or omissions in the exercise of his or

215

her official functions and in other circumstances in which lack of immunity would be inconsistent with diplomatic status. The diplomat is also immune from criminal process and from most civil process in the receiving state. See § 464, Restatement (Third) (1987).

§ 9–2. **Treaties.** Customary international law governing the treatment of diplomatic personnel has been codified in the Convention, ratified by one hundred thirty-two nations by the end of 1984. The agreement protects both diplomatic personnel and property. Its provisions may be summarized as follows (references to articles are to the Convention):

The person of a diplomatic officer is inviolable under international law and the receiving nation has an affirmative duty to protect each diplomat from an attack "on his person, freedom or dignity." Convention, art. 29. Consequently, the receiving nation may neither arrest nor detain the diplomat, and the diplomat is immune from the criminal laws as well as the civil and administrative jurisdiction. Convention, art. 31(1). Diplomatic personnel may not be compelled to give evidence. Convention, art. 31(2). They are also immune from personal service, Convention, art. 35, most taxes, Convention, art. 34, social security provisions, art. 33, and customs duties and inspections, Convention, art. 36. Diplomatic immunity also extends to the diplomat's family members. Convention, art. 37.

The Convention does not, however, grant immunity in: (1) an action concerning private immovable property other than property held in behalf of the sending state for the diplomatic mission; (2) an action for the disposition of an estate in the receiving state with which the diplomatic officer has non-official involvement; or (3) an action involving a diplomatic officer's commercial or professional conduct outside the scope of his official functions. Convention, art. 31(1)(a–c). In addition, diplomats are not exempt from the jurisdiction of the sending state, Convention, art. 31(4). That state may expressly waive the immunity of its diplomatic personnel. Also, the diplomat himself may impliedly waive his immunity to counterclaims in suits that he files in the courts of the receiving state. Convention, art. 32.

The physical premises of a diplomatic mission are also inviolable. Convention, art. 22. The receiving state has an affirmative duty to assist the sending state in obtaining all necessary facilities, Convention, art. 25, and to protect those facilities once they are established. Convention, art. 22. Additionally, the receiving state is under an affirmative obligation to allow the mission freedom of movement, Convention, art. 26, and communication. Convention, art. 27. The mission's premises are free from local taxes, Convention, art. 23, and the receiving state may not tax official fees. Convention, art. 28. The archives of a mission are also inviolable. Convention, art. 24.

In addition to the Vienna Convention on Diplomatic Relations, diplomatic personnel are protected under The Convention on the Prevention and Punishment of Crimes Against Internationally Protected Persons, Including Diplomatic Agents. This convention seeks to deny sanctuary to those who attack, kidnap, or injure diplomatic agents by requiring signatory states to prosecute or extradite the accused party. As of January 1, 1984, sixty-one nations were parties to this convention.

Consular immunity is addressed in the Vienna Convention on Consular Relations which prohibits the arrest or detention of consular officers except for grave crimes and under court decision. Consular Convention, art. 41. Consular officers are not subject to judicial jurisdiction "in respect of acts performed in the exercise of their consular functions," Consular Convention, art. 43, although they may be required to give evidence. Consular Convention, art. 44. These privileges may be waived by the sending state. Consular Convention, art. 45. See § 465, Restatement (Third) (1987).

International civil servants employed by the United Nations enjoy a variety of immunities under the Convention on the Privileges and Immunities of the United Nations. That convention provides generally for immunity from personal arrest and protects papers, documents and courier bags. International civil servants are usually exempted from alien registration acts and generally have personal immunities similar to those accorded diplomats and consuls.

§ **9–3. The Iranian Hostages Case.** The most recent authoritative statement of the international law of diplomatic immunity is found in the Case Concerning United States Diplomatic and Consular Staff in Teheran (United States v. Iran), 1980 ICJ 3. In that case, the United States accused the Iranian Government of seizing embassies and consulates in Iran and of unlawfully detaining U.S. diplomats as hostages. The Court stressed repeatedly that Iran had clearly breached its obligations to the U.S. under both international treaties and general international law. Id., at 30–1, 37–41. More importantly, however, the Court repeatedly declared "[t]he fundamental character of the principle of inviolability," Id. at 40–42. The Court emphasized sharply the basic importance of the rules on diplomatic immunity, id. at 42, which could not be altered by alleged extenuating circumstances. Id. at 41. In this case, the Court, reaffirmed not only the Conventions, but also longstanding customary principles of diplomatic immunity.

§ **9–4. U.S. statutory law.** The United States has enacted the terms of the Vienna Convention on Diplomatic Relations into federal statutory law, 22 U.S.C. § 254a–e (1982), which extends the privileges and immunities of the Convention to *all* diplomatic personnel regardless of whether the sending state is a Convention party. Id. at

§ 254(b). Under the statute, the President may, on
the basis of reciprocity, specify privileges and immunities for diplomatic personnel which are either
more or less favorable than those specified by the
Convention. Id. at § 254(e). The United States
may also require diplomatic missions to insure
themselves against liability for the benefit of parties injured by diplomatic personnel. Purchasing
liability insurance does not constitute a waiver of
immunity under the Convention. Id. at § 254(d).
The United States implemented the provisions of
the Convention on the Prevention and Punishment
of Crimes Against Internationally Protected Persons, Including Diplomatic Agents, in 18 U.S.C.
§ 112, making an attack upon diplomatic personnel a federal offense. Both acts cover consular
officials as well. The International Organizations
Immunities Act, 22 U.S.C. § 258 et seq. provides
protection for international civil servants in the
United States.

§ 9–5. U.S. case law. There is relatively little
recent U.S. case law on diplomatic immunity and
no Supreme Court cases on the subject. The federal courts tend to treat the Convention as a standard matter of treaty interpretation. See e.g.
United States v. Kostadinov, 734 F.2d 905 (2d Cir.
1984); (who is a member of a mission?) Abdulaziz
v. Metropolitan Dade County, 741 F.2d 1328 (11th
Cir.1984) (immunity from suit). In applying the
Convention, the courts will not second guess the
State Department; it alone determines who has

diplomatic status in the United States. United States v. Lumumba, 741 F.2d 12, 15 (2d Cir.1984); Cf. United States v. Palestine Liberation Organization, 695 F.Supp. 1456 (S.D.N.Y.1988).

III. STATE IMMUNITIES

Although both the principles of sovereign immunity and the act of state doctrine have their roots in concepts of sovereignty found in international law, the policies that energize them in the United States are principally those associated with the constitutional principle of separation of powers. Both reflect considerations of international comity and are derived from the recognition that legal confrontations between sovereigns should be avoided whenever possible. They therefore reflect the proposition that where one sovereign has jurisdiction over the person or acts of another, the interests of international harmony and accountability dictate restraint by local decisionmakers. It is for the political branches, not the courts, to decide when such authority will be exercised.

These doctrines also result in part from a conception that equates the exercise of jurisdiction with the application of physical force. Thus, they have their roots also in the elemental peace-preserving function of the international legal system. Because such considerations lie at the heart of these doctrines, these principles indicate *when* existing authority will be exercised rather than whether such authority exists. They are treated in the United States as principles of foreign relations law.

A. Sovereign Immunity

§ 9–6. **Historical development.** The sovereign immunity principle was originally developed to address the problem of concurrent jurisdiction that arises when a foreign sovereign enters a host sovereign's territory, thereby subjecting itself to the host's jurisdiction. Chief Justice John Marshall, writing in the Schooner-Exchange v. McFaddon, 11 U.S. 116 (1812), in deciding that a French warship in a United States port was immune from the jurisdiction of United States courts, concluded that no foreign sovereign would subject itself to the absolute and exclusive power of another without an implied understanding that entry into the foreign territory included a grant of immunity from the territorial sovereign's power. Under this reasoning, the immunity of the foreign sovereign was absolute. This theory, derived from principles of state sovereignty, was viewed as required by customary international law. See Berizzi Bros. v. S.S. Pesaro, 271 U.S. 562 (1926).

In the late 1940s, the sovereign immunity doctrine in United States courts came to be treated as a "political question". Ex parte Peru, 318 U.S. 578, 588–89 (1943). Immunity was granted or denied, not on the basis of an independent judicial analysis of the requirements of international law but rather as the result of recommendations to the courts by the Department of State or, when no such recommendation was forthcoming, on the basis of past State Department practice. Republic of Mexico v. Hoffman, 324 U.S. 30 (1945). The principles that would guide State Department communications about immunity in future cases were stated in The Tate Letter, 26 State Dept. Bull. 984 (1952). In that letter the Legal Advisor's Office informed the Department of Justice that henceforth the State Department would operate under the "restrictive" theory of sovereign immunity, recommending immunity only where the adjudication involved the public acts of a foreign sovereign, (*jure imperii*), not when it involved commercial acts that could be carried on by private parties (*jure gestionis*). If the State Department made no recommendation of immunity the characterization "governmental" or "commercial" was to be determined by the courts. To make this determination, courts looked to the nature or the purpose of the acts in question. National City Bank v. Republic of China, 348 U.S. 356 (1955).

In Victory Transport, Inc. v. Comisaria General, 336 F.2d 354 (2d Cir.1964), the Second Circuit held that the Spanish government's chartering a ship to move surplus grain from the United States to Spain for distribution to the Spanish people was a private commercial act, and that the defendant was not immune from suit to compel arbitration as required by the charter party, although it was an arm of the Spanish government. The court identified five categories of acts generally treated under public international law as being governmental in nature: (a) internal administrative acts, such as expulsion of an alien; (b) legislative acts, such as nationalization; (c) acts concerning the armed forces; (d) acts concerning diplomatic activity; and (e) public loans. Id. at 360. The majority of the world's nations recognize the restrictive theory, with some variations. A few other nations, particularly the state trading countries, continue to follow the absolute theory, a result clearly encouraged by self-interest.

Given the diplomatic pressures brought to bear on the State Department to recommend immunity in cases involving foreign sovereigns and the political difficulties that arose when such recommendations were refused, it was virtually impossible for the Department to follow the restrictive theory consistently in determining whether to recommend immunity in specific cases. See, e.g., Rich v. Naviera Vacuba, S.A., 295 F.2d 24 (4th Cir.1961); Chemical Natural Resources, Inc. v. Republic of Venezuela, 420 Pa. 134, 215 A.2d 864 (1966), cert. denied, 385 U.S. 822 (1966). Efforts to hold administrative-style hearings to determine immunity did not alleviate the problem. Consequently, the Foreign Sovereign Immunities Act of 1976, (hereinafter FSIA) 90 Stat. 2891, 28 U.S.C. §§ 1602–1611, was adopted to eliminate the State Department's control over results in sovereign immunity cases and to permit the judiciary to determine immunity solely as a matter of law.

§ 9–7. The Foreign Sovereign Immunities Act (FSIA). The intent of Congress in passing the FSIA (all sections cited refer to this act), was to codify the restrictive theory of sovereign immunity. See International Ass'n of Machinist and Aerospace Workers v. Organization of Petroleum Exporting Countries, 649 F.2d 1354 (9th Cir.1981). Therefore, the Act does not apply to causes of action arising before The Tate Letter in 1952. p. 214, supra. Jackson v. The People's Republic of China, 794 F.2d 1490 (11th Cir. 1986). Essentially the Act preserves immunity from suit for all foreign sovereigns, § 1604, except in certain limited circumstances. See § 1604 (international agreements to which the U.S. is a party prior to the enactment of the FSIA may provide for no immunity); § 1605 (list of exceptions in the FSIA discussed infra); § 1607 (counterclaims). In addition the Act provides explicit procedures for serving process and obtaining personal jurisdiction over foreign states. § 1608.

The definition of a "foreign state" under the FSIA includes any of its political subdivisions, agencies, or instrumentalities. § 1603(a). Agencies and instrumentalities are defined as any "separate legal entity, corporate or otherwise," which is either an organ of or owned by a foreign state and which is neither a citizen of one of the United States or of any third nation. § 1603(b).

The most controversial sections of the FSIA are the specified exceptions to immunity in §§ 1605 and 1607. This is especially so because it is the party claiming the immunity who has the burden of demonstrating that the exceptions in the Act do not apply. Arango v. Guzman Travel Advisers, 621 F.2d 1371, 1378 (5th Cir.1980).

a. *Jurisdiction.* The FSIA is the sole basis for obtaining jurisdiction over a foreign state in United States courts. Argentine Republic v. Amerada Hess Shipping Corp., 109 S.Ct. 683, 688, 690 (1989). Considerations related to subject-matter jurisdiction and personal jurisdiction are merged under the FSIA. § 1330(a) grants subject matter jurisdiction for "any nonjury civil action against a foreign state" in which the foreign state is not entitled to immunity. § 1330(b) grants personal jurisdiction if the court has jurisdiction under § 1330(a) *and* service of process has been made under § 1608.

Congress intended that the immunity provisions creating subject matter jurisdiction include the contacts necessary for personal jurisdiction. Therefore, if one of the exceptions specified in the FSIA applies, a district court will have subject-matter jurisdiction. If the exceptions do not apply, the court lacks such jurisdiction. Thus, actions brought under the FSIA "arise under" a federal statute and the federal courts may properly exercise jurisdiction. Since there is no limitation as to the plaintiff's citizenship, a foreign plaintiff may bring an action against a foreign defendant. Verlinden B.V. v. Central Bank of Nigeria, 461 U.S. 480 (1983).

Actions under the Act may be brought initially in either state or federal court, but a foreign state is guaranteed the right to remove a civil action from state to federal court. 28 U.S.C. § 1441. Finally, the FSIA, provides absolute immunity for property protected by the International Organizations Immunities Act for property owned by the central bank of a foreign state, § 1611(b)(1) and for military property. § 1611(b)(2).

b. *Waivers of Immunity.* A foreign state will be subject to jurisdiction if it has either impliedly or expressly waived its immunity. Once a waiver is made, it cannot be withdrawn except in a manner consistant with the terms of the waiver. § 1605(a) (1).

An explicit waiver of immunity occurs when a foreign state waives immunity by treaty or by a contract with a private party. An implicit waiver may occur when a foreign state agrees to arbitration in another country knowing that U.S. courts can compel or enforce such arbitration, agrees that the law of another country will govern a contract, or engages in any of the activities enumerated in the FSIA. Sovereign immunity may also be waived by a failure to raise it as a defense in the first responsive pleading.

c. *Commercial activities.* The FSIA denies immunity in actions arising out of the foreign state's commercial activities if those activities are performed in the U.S. or if they produce direct effects in the U.S. § 1605(a)(2). For the purposes of the

FSIA a commercial activity may be regular conduct or an individual transaction so long as its nature rather than its purpose is the determining factor. § 1603(d). Commercial activities of foreign states are not sovereign acts within the meaning of the FSIA. West v. Multibanco Comermex, 807 F.2d 820 (9th Cir.1987).

The courts have interpreted this section of the statute in light of its legislative history, prior case law, and the standards of international law. Texas Trading & Milling Corp. v. Federal Republic of Nigeria, 647 F.2d 300, 309–10 (2d Cir.1981). A court first defines the act and activity involved; then determines whether the act or activity falls within the definition; and finally characterizes the act or activity as either commercial or governmental. Id.

Acts characterized as governmental include: the granting and revocation of a license to export a natural resource, MOL, Inc. v. Peoples Republic of Bangladesh, 736 F.2d 1326 (9th Cir.1984), the negligence of a plane manufacturer which caused a plane crash overseas, killing the U.S. pilot (there being no direct effect in the United States), Australian Gov't Aircraft Factories v. Lynne, 743 F.2d 672 (9th Cir.1984), the supervision of an office and personnel by an international health organization, Tuck v. Pan American Health Organization, 668 F.2d 547 (D.C.Cir.1981); and exploration by a government owned oil company.

Activities characterized as commercial include purchasing cement and issuing letters of credit, see Texas Trading, supra, and chartering a ship to deliver grain from a United States food grain program to a wholly-owned foreign state-company. Gemini Shipping, Inc. v. Foreign Trade Organization for Chemicals and Foodstuff, 647 F.2d 317 (2d Cir.1981). In addition some courts require a nexus between the commercial act and the plaintiff's cause of action. See Vencedora Oceanica Navigacion v. Compagnie Nationale Algerienne De Navigation (C.N.A.N.), 730 F.2d 195, 200 (5th Cir.1984) (and cases cited).

d. *Expropriation claims.* A foreign state is not immune when "rights in property taken in violation of international law are in issue." § 1605(a) (3). This includes suits involving property nationalized or expropriated without compensation, and arbitrary or discriminatory takings. For this exception to apply, the property must be present in the United States in connection with a commercial activity being carried on by the foreign state; or owned or operated by an agency or instrumentality (of the foreign state) involved in commercial activity in the United States. Id.

e. *Rights in property in the U.S.* Immunity will be denied when rights in immovable property (real estate), inherited, or gift property located in the United States are in issue. § 1605(a)(4). Property interests in real estate include "leasehold, easements, or servitudes, possessory rights [for] rights to payment of money secured by an interest in land." The interest must be such that the title to, or the use of, the lands will be affected by the outcome of the action. To be covered by this exception plaintiff's claims must affect possessory rights or property interests in land located in the U.S. See Asociacion de Reclamantes v. United Mexican States, 735 F.2d 1517 (D.C.Cir.1984).

f. *Noncommercial torts.* A state is not immune in tort actions involving money damages where the tort occurred in the United States, § 1605(a)(5), including actions for personal injury, death, and loss or damage to property caused by a tortious act or omission of the foreign state or its agents. Id. A state will remain immune, however, if the tort claim is based upon the discharge of a discretionary function; § 1605(a)(5)(A), or if it arises from "malicious prosecution, abuse of process, libel, slander, misrepresentation, deceit or interference with contract rights." § 1605(a)(5)(B). Although the exception is cast in terms sufficiently general to make it applicable to a variety of situations, the legislative history suggests that the provision was intended to address traffic accidents caused by automobiles operated by foreign embassy personnel, Persinger v. Islamic Republic of Iran, 729 F.2d 835, 840 (D.C.Cir.1984). The Supreme Court has held that the exception "is limited by its terms . . . to those cases in which the damage to or loss of property occurs in the United States." Argentine Republic v. Amerada Hess Shipping Corp., 109

S.Ct. 683, 690 (1989) (emphasis by the Court); see Olson v. United Mexican States, 729 F.2d 641, 645 (9th Cir.1984), cert. denied, 469 U.S. 917 (1984). The phrase "within the United States" means within "the continental United States and those islands that are part of the United States or its possessions." Id. at 691. See Persinger, supra, at 842, U.S. embassies are not within this exception because the ground on which an embassy stands remains the territory of the receiving state. Mc-Keel v. Islamic Republic of Iran, 722 F.2d 582, 588 (9th Cir.1983), cert. denied, 469 U.S. 880 (1984).

When determining whether an act is "discretionary," acts at the planning level are distinguished from acts at the operational level. The former are discretionary while the latter are not. In making this determination courts will also examine the ability of United States courts to evaluate the act, and the impact that such an evaluation might have on relations with the foreign government. Id. at 647.

g. *Maritime liens.* Under § 1606, a foreign state is not immune from suits brought in admiralty to enforce a maritime lien against a vessel (or cargo), which is owned by the foreign state, when the lien is based on the commercial activity of the foreign state, § 1605(b), subject to compliance with the notice requirements provided in the Act. § 1605(b) & (c). Such admiralty claims will be treated as *in personam* actions, with the value of the vessel or cargo at the time the lien arose being the ceiling for any judgment. § 1605(b).

h. *Liability.* If a foreign state is not entitled to immunity from jurisdiction, it is liable to the same extent as if it were a private party. State Bank of India v. NLRB, 808 F.2d 526 (7th Cir.1986). A foreign state will not be subject to punitive damages except in a wrongful death action where the law of the state in which the act occurred provides only punitive damages. In these cases, the foreign state will nonetheless be liable for the actual or compensatory damages incurred by the parties injured by the death. § 1606. Harris v. Polskie Linie Lotnicze, 820 F.2d 1000 (9th Cir.1987).

i. *Counterclaims.* When a foreign state brings an action in a state or federal court, immunity will be denied in regard to counterclaims against the state if the foreign state would not have been immune had the claim been brought as a direct claim, the claim arises from the transaction or occurrence that is the subject matter of the foreign state's claim or the counterclaim does not seek relief in excess of, or differing from, the amount sought by the foreign state. § 1607.

j. *Attachment and execution.* The property of a foreign state is immune from attachment, arrest or execution unless otherwise provided by international agreement. § 1609. Such immunity is not accorded, however, where the foreign state has waived its immunity, where the property attached was used in the United States in the commercial activity which is the basis of the claim, the judgment to be executed is based on property rights taken in violation of international law, the property was acquired by accession or gift, is immovable property located in the U.S. or represents the proceeds of liability insurance procured by the foreign state for itself or its employees. § 1610(a). See City of Englewood v. Socialist People's Libyan Arab Jamahiriya, 773 F.2d 31 (3d Cir.1985).

Agencies or instrumentalities of the foreign state lose immunity under the same conditions as the state itself. In addition, they are not immune if the underlying claim lacks immunity under certain provisions of § 1605, whether or not the property sought to be attached was used in the activity in question. Prejudgment attachment is prohibited as a means of obtaining jurisdiction but may be used to assure satisfaction of an eventually successful claim or where there has been an explicit waiver by the foreign state. § 1610(d).

For a more detailed description of all aspects of the law of sovereign immunity, see §§ 451–463 Restatement (Third) (1987).

B. Act of State

§ **9–8. Historical development.** The act of state doctrine is closely related to the principle of sovereign immunity. In England, the term was used to characterize the Crown's adoption of a private citizen's act abroad against a foreigner as an act of the state, thereby retroactively affording the citizen effective immunity against civil suit. See, e.g., Johnstone v. Pedlar, [1921] 2 A.C. 262 (H.L.).

a. *Early cases.* The United States version of the doctrine was originally applied in two early cases to dismiss suits against former foreign government officials for acts done in their official capacity. Hatch v. Baez, 7 Hun. 596 (N.Y.App.Div. 1876); Underhill v. Hernandez, 168 U.S. 250 (1897). In *Underhill* the Court stated the doctrine:

> Every sovereign State is bound to respect the independence of every other sovereign State, and the courts of one country will not sit in judgment on the acts of the government of another done within its own territory. Redress of grievances by reason of such acts must be obtained through the means open to be availed of by sovereign powers as between themselves. Id. at 252.

Later cases either suggested that the doctrine was required by principles of comity, Oetjen v. Central Leather Co., 246 U.S. 297 (1918), Ricaud v. American Metal Co., 246 U.S. 304 (1918), or treated it as a special choice of law rule growing logically from the vested rights theory of conflict of laws. American Banana Co. v. United Fruit Co., 213 U.S. 347 (1909).

b. *The Bernstein exception.* Modern decisions treat the act of state doctrine as an element of federal common law, designed to avoid interference with the executive's conduct of foreign relations while protecting the integrity of the judicial role.

Banco Nacional de Cuba v. Sabbatino, 376 U.S. 398, 425 (1964). The doctrine's role to avoid exacerbating international relations was recognized in Bernstein v. Van Heyghen Freres, 163 F.2d 246 (2d Cir.1947). In *Bernstein,* Judge Learned Hand applied the doctrine *after* Germany had been defeated during the war to refuse to set aside the coerced taking of property from the Jewish plaintiff by Nazi officials. The court changed its position when, in a later identical case, Bernstein v. Nederlandsche-Amerikaansche Stoomvaart–Maatschappij, 210 F.2d 375 (2d Cir.1954), the State Department informed it by letter that United States' foreign relations did not require judicial abstention in cases involving Nazi confiscations. Under this so-called "*Bernstein* exception," the act of state doctrine would not be applied when the State Department explicitly indicated that the conduct of United States foreign relations did not require it.

§ **9–9. Recent Supreme Court decisions.** The current form and content of the act of state doctrine was developed in a series of U.S. Supreme Court cases decided between 1964 and 1976. In the *Sabbatino* case, supra, the Court invoked it to refuse to adjudicate the validity of an uncompensated Cuban taking of American owned property in the face of lower court holdings that the doctrine did not apply when the foreign act of state violated international law. The Court reaffirmed that the doctrine was grounded in concepts of separation powers with "constitutional underpinnings" but applied it (with the support of the executive branch as *amicus*) because to adjudicate the case would impinge on both the executive and the judicial power. Since the government had taken the public position that the Cuban takings were illegal because uncompensated, an objective adjudication risked serious embarrassment to the executive branch because the international law concerning the compensation requirement was unclear. On the other hand, to permit an ostensibly objective adjudication to be controlled by considerations of United States national interest would pervert the judicial role. Justice Harlan summarized the holding as follows:

. . . [w]e decide only that the Judicial Branch will not examine the validity of a taking of property within its own territory by a foreign sovereign government, extant and recognized by this country at the time of suit, in the absence of a treaty or other unambiguous agreement regarding controlling legal principles, even if the complaint alleges that the taking violated customary international law. 376 U.S. at 428. See § 443, Restatement (Third) (1987).

These separation of powers concerns did not impress the Congress. In the so-called *Sabbatino* Amendment to the Foreign Assistance Act of 1964, 78 Stat. 1013, 22 U.S.C. § 2370(e)(2), Congress required courts in the United States to adjudicate claims that property had been taken in violation of international law. The amendment virtually ordered the courts to find a violation if "full, adequate and prompt" compensation had not been paid for the expropriation unless the executive branch informed the court that it was in the interests of the United States to apply the act of state doctrine and refuse adjudication. The government made no such request in the *Sabbatino* case on remand, and the lower court found the Cuban taking invalid. The statute reversed the effect of the Supreme Court's decision. Banco Nacional de Cuba v. Farr, Whitlock & Co., 383 F.2d 166 (2d Cir. 1967). Subsequent cases have construed the *Sabbatino* Amendment narrowly to limit its effect to situations where the property whose title is in dispute is physically present in the United States and have followed the act of state rationale as found in Supreme Court's *Sabbatino* opinion.

In First National City Bank v. Banco Nacional de Cuba, 406 U.S. 759 (1972), the Court agreed to adjudicate the validity of a Cuban taking of Citibank's property as part of a counterclaim when the Department of State wrote to the Court that the act of state doctrine need not apply. While a majority of the Court found the doctrine inapplicable, only a minority were willing to recognize the *Bernstein* exception and treat the Executive's suggestion as conclusive. The tone of the Department's letter had suggested that finding the taking invalid was almost a foregone conclusion. As in *Sabbatino,* a principal concern was to protect the integrity of the judicial process and to avoid giving the appearance of even-handed adjudication when

the results were dictated in fact by the requirements of United States foreign policy.

Finally, in Alfred Dunhill of London, Inc. v.
Republic of Cuba, 425 U.S. 682 (1976), the Department of State wrote what could be termed a general *Bernstein* letter that questioned the need for the
act of state doctrine in any circumstances and
suggested that adjudication of cases of this kind
would not injure United States foreign relations.
The Court retained the doctrine but four justices
argued that it did not apply to a foreign sovereign's
commercial acts, even though those acts were done
within its own territory. Such acts are immune
from examination in United States courts only if
United States law is inapplicable under international jurisdictional principles.

The current status of the *Bernstein* exception to
the act of state doctrine is unclear. The Court in
Sabbatino expressly avoided endorsing it, even
though that case presented an opportunity to do so,
and a majority of the Court questioned its continued vitality in *Citibank*. The Court also rejected a
statement by the executive branch in *Dunhill* that
the act of state doctrine itself was no longer necessary for United States foreign policy.

§ 9–10. The "phenomenological" rule. The
Second Circuit, attempting to make sense out of
these signals, adopted what it termed a "phenomenological rule" by adding together the multiple
holdings in *Citibank*. Under that rule, where the
executive branch has provided a *Bernstein* letter

and there is no showing that adjudication will interfere with foreign relations and the claim against the foreign sovereign is asserted as a counterclaim for no more than a set-off, then the act of state doctrine will not bar adjudication. Banco Nacional de Cuba v. Chase Manhattan Bank, 658 F.2d 875, 884 (2d Cir.1981). (See also Empresa Cubana Exportadora, Inc. v. Lamborn & Co., 652 F.2d 231 (2d Cir.1981) where the absence of a communication from the executive was treated as an indication that the act of state doctrine was properly applied in the case.) However, the court in Banco Nacional de Cuba v. Chemical Bank New York Trust Co., 594 F.Supp. 1553 (S.D.N.Y.1984), treated the lack of a *Bernstein* letter as irrelevant in view of "public statements made by the State Department [expressing] executive branch approval of judicial intervention." Id. at 1564. Judge Brieant took the position that any public utterance by the State Department could serve to relieve the courts from any constraint upon the exercise of jurisdiction. Id. at 1563–64. But compare Environmental Techtronics v. W.S. Kirkpatrick, Inc., 847 F.2d 1052 (3d Cir.1988). He went on to conclude that equitable principles would permit the defendant to set off any losses Chemical Bank had incurred because of the Cuban expropriations in question against Banco Nacional's claims. Id. at 1565; See First National City Bank v. Banco Para el Comercio Exterior de Cuba (Bancec), 462 U.S. 611 (1983).

§ 9–11. **The treaty exception.** The so-called "treaty law exception," referred to by Justice Harlan in *Sabbatino,* was applied in Kalamazoo Spice Extraction Co. v. Provisional Military Government of Ethiopia, 729 F.2d 422 (6th Cir.1984). In that case the court was asked to decide a counterclaim by an American defendant for the expropriation of his property by the revolutionary government of Ethiopia. The 1953 Treaty of Amity and Economic Relations Between the United States and Ethiopia, included a standard of "prompt payment of just and effective compensation" in the event that one party expropriated property belonging to nationals of the other. The District Court applied the act of state doctrine and dismissed the case. Before the appeal was heard, Davis R. Robinson, Legal Advisor the Department of State, transmitted a letter to the Sixth Circuit in which he wrote

When, as in this case, there is a controlling legal standard for compensation, we believe that adjudication would not be inconsistent with foreign policy interests under the Act of State Doctrine.

On appeal, the Sixth Circuit accepted the Robinson position, expressed in the government's *amicus* brief, that the treaty exception applied. Not only was the legal standard concerning compensation clear, but the government's brief indicated that foreign policy concerns would not require judicial abstention in this case. It is not clear at present whether the courts will apply the "treaty exception" without a special letter in each case to indicate the Executive's view of the case at bar.

§ **9–12. Situs of property.** The doctrine does not apply to attempts by governments to take property located outside their territory. In these cases, the forum court may refuse to give effect to the attempted taking because to do so would be contrary to the forum's public policy. Republic of Iraq v. First National City Bank, 241 F.Supp. 567 (S.D.N.Y.1965), affirmed, 353 F.2d 47 (2d Cir.1965), cert. denied, 382 U.S. 1027 (1966). The forum may recognize the validity of the foreign act of state as to property located in the United States, if to do so furthers U.S. policy. United States v. Belmont, 301 U.S. 324 (1937), Banco Nacional de Cuba v. Chemical Bank New York Trust Co., 658 F.2d 903 (2d Cir.1981). Situs questions become particularly important in cases involving seizure of intangibles. Whether such situs is determined under federal common law as a necessary corollary to the act of state doctrine or under state choice of law rules is not clear. See Allied Bank International v. Banco Credito Agricola de Cartago, 733 F.2d 23 (2d Cir. 1984), reversed on rehearing, 757 F.2d 516 (2d Cir. 1984).

§ **9–13. Act of state in antitrust.** Perhaps the most controversial application of the act of state doctrine in United States courts is in the antitrust cases. In these cases, the act of state doctrine is usually raised by defendant in a private treble damage action claiming that any injury to plaintiff was caused by the act of a foreign government, not by defendants' combination or conspiracy. In Hunt v. Mobil Oil Co., 550 F.2d 68 (2d Cir.1977), cert. denied, 434 U.S. 984 (1977), for example, the defendant oil companies successfully urged that the plaintiff's injury was due solely to the confiscation of plaintiff's oil property by the Libyan Government. The court refused to examine Libya's motives to determine whether the confiscation had been encouraged by the defendants on the grounds that to do so would risk exactly the harm to United States foreign relations that the act of state doctrine was intended to avoid. Contra: Environmental Tectonics v. W.S. Kirkpatrick, 847 F.2d 1052, 1061 (3d Cir.1988) (dealing with RICO).

If the foreign government has not caused plaintiff's injury, its bare participation in anticompetitive activity will not make the antitrust laws inapplicable to the private defendants involved. Compare, American Banana Co. v. United Fruit Co., 213 U.S. 347 (1909) with Continental Ore Co. v. Union Carbide & Carbon Corp., 370 U.S. 690 (1962) and United States v. Sisal Sales Corp., 274 U.S. 268 (1927). See Timberlane Lumber Co. v. Bank of America, 549 F.2d 597 (9th Cir.1976); Occidental Petroleum Corp. v. Buttes Oil, 331 F.Supp. 92 (C.D. Cal.1971), (affirmed per curiam adopting district court's op.), 461 F.2d 1261 (9th Cir.1972).

CHAPTER 10

INTERNATIONAL LEGAL RESEARCH SOURCES

I. INTRODUCTION

Chapter 2, supra, deals with the formal sources and evidence of international law. This chapter introduces the research tools and methods that international lawyers employ when they search for specific authority on a given point of law. The presentation assumes that the reader has an understanding of the conceptual framework and sources of international law described in Chapter 2.

II. TREATISES AND OTHER SCHOLARLY MATERIAL

§ **10–1. Treatises.** Treatises are the most useful starting point for research in international law. These books, usually written by leading scholars in the field, provide an analytical exposition of the law and contain extensive citations to all relevant authorities. Such treatises exist in many languages and translations. The following are the principal English-language treatises:

I. Brownlie, *Principles of Public International Law* (3d ed. 1979).

Oppenheim's International Law: A Treatise (H. Lauterpacht, vol. 1, 8th ed. 1955, vol. 2, 7th ed. 1952).

D. P. O'Connell, *International Law* (2d ed. 1970), 2 vols.

G. Schwarzenberger, *International Law* as Applied by International Courts and Tribunals (vol. 1, 3d ed. 1957, vol. 2, 1968, vol. 3, 1976, vol. 4, 1986).

M. Sorensen, *Manual of Public International Law* (1968).

Many shorter, albeit less comprehensive, international law texts are also available and provide useful introductions to the field. Among these are the following books:

M. B. Akehurst, *A Modern Introduction to International Law* (6th ed. 1987);

J. L. Brierly, *The Law of Nations* (H. Waldock, 6th ed. 1963). This classic one-volume work, although in need of updating, remains a valuable and highly readable overview of the subject);

D. W. Greig, *International Law* (2d ed. 1976);

M. W. Janis, *An Introduction to International Law* (1988).

W. Levi, *Contemporary International Law* (1979);

J. G. Starke, *An Introduction to International Law* (9th ed. 1984).

In addition to the above-mentioned works, which provide a comprehensive overview of or an introduction to international law, there are many specialized books dealing with individual topics or areas. The principal monographs on any of these subjects will usually be cited in the treatises referred to above.

§ **10–2. Encyclopedias and Restatements.** Professor R. Bernhardt is now editing the first comprehensive English-language *Encyclopedia of Public International Law* under the auspices of the Max-Planck Institute for Comparative Public Law and International Law of Heidelberg, West Germany. The first installment volume of this work was published in 1981. Eleven installment volumes have appeared since that date; the remaining ones are scheduled to be completed by the end of 1991. Each of the 1200 odd essays of the *Encyclopedia,* written by leading international legal scholars and practitioners from many parts of the world, provides a concise and most useful overview of the topic in question and a selected bibliography.

The American Law Institute (ALI), which has over the years published various Restatements of the Law, adopted in 1965 the *Restatement (Second) on the Foreign Relations Law of the United States.* Although forming part of the *Restatement (Second)* series, no earlier official version was ever published. In the late 1970's, the ALI authorized the preparation of a new Restatement. Known as the *Restatement (Third) on the Foreign Relations Law of the United States,* it was published in 1987 in a two-volume set. The *Restatement* is a highly valued international law research tool. U.S. courts generally view it as the most authoritative scholarly statement of contemporary international law.

The *Restatement* deals with public international law and the relevant American law bearing on the application of international law in and by the U.S. Each section consists of a statement of the black letter law, followed by comments and reporters' notes. The latter are particularly useful because of their careful analysis of and citations to the relevant international law authorities. Unlike the comments, the reporters' notes state the views of the reporters only and their substance is not endorsed as such by the ALI.

§ 10–3. Yearbooks of the International Law Commission. The activities of the International Law Commission of the United Nations, see Chapter 3, § 3–7 and Chapter II, § 2–7, supra, are described in its *Yearbooks*. This publication reproduces, *inter alia,* the studies and reports of the Commission's rapporteurs on the various international law subjects under consideration by that body. Many of these studies are comprehensive legal monographs of great practical and scholarly authority. They are consequently a valuable resource for international lawyers. On the activities of the International Law Commission generally, see the latest edition of the UN publication entitled *The Work of the International Law Commission.* See also, McCaffrey, "The Fortieth Session of the International Law Commission," 83 Am.J.Int'l

L. 153 (1989). Similar studies are also prepared
from time to time under the auspices of non-governmental legal groups such as the International
Law Association and the prestigious Institut de
Droit International.

§ **10–4. Casebooks.** These works can be useful
reference tools for international law research. Besides reproducing the major international and national judicial decisions dealing with international
law questions, casebooks usually also contain extensive notes, comments and valuable bibliographic
information. The following are among the major
American casebooks:

W. Bishop, *International Law: Cases and Materials* (3d ed. 1971).

L. Henkin, Pugh, Schachter and Smit, *International Law: Cases and Materials* (2d ed. 1987).

M. McDougal and Reisman, *International Law in
Contemporary Perspective: the Public Order of
the World Community (1981).*

H. Steiner and Vagts, *Transnational Legal Problems*: Materials and Text (3d ed. 1986).

J. Sweeney, Oliver and Leech, *Cases and Materials on the International Legal System* (3d ed.
1988).

B. Weston, Falk and D'Amato, *International Law
and World Order: A Problem Oriented Casebook*
(Rev. ed. 1982).

These books are periodically updated. They
reproduce, in separate document supplements, the

texts of major international agreements and other materials of importance. The supplements themselves are, consequently, a useful source of sometimes hard to find information and documentation.

In addition to international law casebooks of a general type, more and more specialized casebooks are now also being published. These deal with a variety of subjects, including international trade and finance, international organizations, human rights, the European Community, world order, etc. In many instances, these books are more comprehensive in scope and hence more useful as research aids than some of the monographs on the same topic.

§ 10–5. **Periodical literature.** For research involving contemporary international law issues it is imperative to check the periodical literature on the subject. Articles dealing with international topics appear not only in the many specialized international law journals published in the U.S. and abroad, but also in general law reviews.

Articles published in American, British and some Commonwealth law journals are indexed in the *Index to Legal Periodicals* and the *Current Law Index*. Material on international law appearing in foreign journals and in a selected number of American reviews are noted in the *Index to Foreign Legal Periodicals*. An even more comprehensive bibliographic guide, published by the Max Planck Institute for Comparative Public Law and International Law, is *Public International Law: A Current*

Bibliography of Articles. It provides access to more than 1000 journals and collected works from all parts of the world.

The leading American law review on the subject is the *American Journal of International Law,* which is edited by a group of well-known scholars and practitioners. A more practice-oriented journal, published by the International Law Section of the American Bar Association, is *The International Lawyer.* In addition, an increasing number of American law schools publish student-edited international legal journals.

The following are some of the more prestigious foreign journals and yearbooks of international law:

Annuaire Francais de Droit International;

Australian Yearbook of International Law;

British Yearbook of International Law;

Canadian Yearbook of International Law;

German Yearbook of International Law;

International and Comparative Law Quarterly;

Netherlands International Law Review;

Zeitschrift für ausländisches öffentliches Recht und Völkerrecht.

Here it is worth noting that many foreign-language international law journals publish a significant number of articles in English. Hence, the mere fact that a citation to an article points to a German, Dutch or Belgian international law review, for example, does not exclude the possibility that the piece appears in English. Where this is not the case, moreover, English summaries are at times provided. Foreign international law journals as a rule also reproduce or summarize decisions of national tribunals, legislation and governmental pronouncements of interest to international lawyers.

Some of the most important essays on contemporary international law questions appear in the *Recueil des Cours* of the Hague Academy of International Law. The Recueil reprints the course lectures by leading international lawyers given at the Hague Academy. These lectures are reproduced either in French or English and usually contain extensive bibliographies.

III. INTERNATIONAL AGREEMENTS

§ **10–6. Treaty collections.** The most comprehensive English-language collection of the texts of international agreements concluded since the World War II is the *United Nations Treaty Series.* It is the successor to the *League of Nations Treaty Series,* which began in 1920. A fine collection of international agreements antedating the League of Nations is the *Consolidated Treaty Series,* edited by Professor Clive Perry.

The *United Nations Treaty Series,* although more comprehensive than any other contemporary treaty collection, is years behind schedule in publishing the treaty texts. The UN is even more behind schedule in the publication of the relevant indices, which means that the researcher is often forced to embark on a very time-consuming volume-by-volume search for a treaty text.   Important recent international agreements are frequently reproduced in *International Legal Materials,* a bi-monthly publication of the American Society of International Law.   The *ILM* usually publishes some important agreements even before they have entered into force.

United States Treaties and Other International Agreements, an official U.S. Government publication, contains the texts of international agreements to which the U.S. is a party.   Until 1950, treaties ratified by the U.S. were published in *Statutes-at-Large.*

§ **10–7. Treaty information.**   The annual Department of State publication *Treaties in Force: A List of Treaties and Other International Agreements of the United States* is an invaluable tool for locating treaties to which the U.S. is a party.   This work permits the researcher to determine, *inter alia,* what treaty relations the U.S. has with individual nations.   Even more current treaty information relating to the U.S. can be found in the monthly *Department of State Bulletin* and in the ILM.

The United Nations publishes the very useful *Multilateral Treaties in Respect of which the Secretary-General Performs Depositary Functions.*   This publication appears annually and contains information about the status of and parties to these agreements. Updated monthly information on the same subject can be found in the *United Nations Chronicle.* Foreign international law journals, particularly the yearbooks, are also a useful resource for treaty information concerning specific countries.

IV. JUDICIAL AND ARBITRAL DECISIONS

§ 10–8. **International court reports.** The International Court of Justice and the various permanent regional international courts publish official collections of their decisions. The International Court of Justice publishes its rulings in a volume entitled *Reports of Judgments, Advisory Opinions and Orders.* Other materials relating to the ICJ proceedings are issued in *Pleadings, Oral Arguments and Documents.* Further information relating to the work of the ICJ and its jurisdiction can be found in the *Yearbook of the International Court of Justice.* The Permanent Court of International Justice followed a publication practice similar to that of the ICJ, but used one series for judgments and another for advisory opinions.

Decisions of the Court of Justice of the European Communities are found in the official *Reports of Cases before the Court.* Unofficial commercial collections published in England (*Common Market Law Reports*) and the U.S. (*CCH Common Market Reports*) are also available.

The European Court of Human Rights publishes two series of materials: *Series A, Judgments and Decisions* and *Series B, Pleadings, Oral Arguments and Documents*. Decisions of the European Court and the European Commission of Human Rights are also reproduced in the *Yearbook of the European Convention of Human Rights*. The *Yearbook* does not always reprint material in full, however. Both the Court and Commission also publish mimeographed reports of their decisions and press releases, which can be obtained from the Council of Europe.

Until recently, the Inter-American Court of Human Rights used a two-series approach similar to that of its European counterpart; namely, *Series A: Judgments and Opinions* and *Series B: Pleadings, Oral Arguments and Documents*. In 1987 it added a third series, entitled *Series C: Decisions and Judgments*. Decisions of the Inter-American Court and Commission of Human Rights are also published in their separate *Annual Reports to the OAS General Assembly* and in the commercially published multi-volume looseleaf collection, *Human Rights: The Inter-American System*, edited by T. Buergenthal and R. Norris.

The *American Journal of International Law* and *International Legal Materials* often reprint or summarize important decisions of the International Court of Justice and of other tribunals. A specialized publication, *Human Rights Law Journal*, reproduces major decisions of the European and In-

ter-American human rights tribunals and of other
international human rights bodies. Other specialized reviews follow a similar practice.

§ 10–9. **International arbitral tribunals.**
The most comprehensive collection of decisions of
international arbitral tribunals is the United Nations publication *Reports of International Arbitral
Awards,* where selected decisions rendered since
the 1890's are reproduced. Other early collections
are those compiled by J.B. Scott, *Hague Court
Reports* (Series 1, 1916 and Series 2, 1932), and J.B.
Moore, *International Arbitrations* (1898). Important current arbitral decisions are reprinted in
International Legal Materials.

§ 10–10. **National court decisions.** *International Law Reports* and its predecessor, the *Annual
Digest and Report of Public International Law
Cases* are the best sources for finding national
court decisions dealing with international law issues. Important domestic decisions are reported in
the various national yearbooks and international
law journals of different countries. *International
Legal Materials* is highly selective in publishing
national court decisions, limiting itself for the most
part to U.S. cases.

V. STATE AND INTERNATIONAL
ORGANIZATION PRACTICE

§ 10–11. **Digests and repertories of practice.**
Governmental pronouncements and official posi-
tions on questions of international law play a vital

role in the creation of customary international law.
See Chapter 2, § 2–3, supra. Evidence of this
practice is, therefore, carefully collected by foreign
offices and/or legal scholars in different countries.
In the U.S., the Department of State has periodically issued analytical digests in which the U.S.
practice is compiled. The latest such work is
Marjorie M. Whiteman's 15-volume *Digest of International Law* (1963–73). An annual volume, *Digest of United States Practice in International Law,*
updates the Whiteman *Digest* with a publications
lag of a few years. Every issue of the *American
Journal of International Law* contains a special
section, usually edited by an attorney on the staff
of the Office of the Legal Adviser of the State
Department, which reports on the *Contemporary
Practice of the United States Relating to International Law.* This report, although necessarily selective, does help to bridge the gap that results
from the delay in the publication of the annual
practice volume.

J.B. Moore and G.H. Hackworth edited earlier
U.S. digests. The latter's eight volumes, published
between 1940 and 1944, cover U.S. international
law practice for much of the first part of this
century. The prior practice is compiled in Moore's
eight-volume digest published in 1906. Similar
works, sometimes denominated repertories of practice, are available for various countries, including,
inter alia, France, Canada, Brazil and the United
Kingdom. Current material can often also be

found in the international law journals and year-books of individual countries. The foreign offices of many nations publish collections of diplomatic history and correspondence, which may also be useful to international lawyers. The basic U.S. publication on this subject is the series entitled *Foreign Relations of the United States.*

§ **10–12. UN practice.** The legally relevant practice of the United Nations is periodically recorded in the official multi-volume *Repertory of Practice of United Nations Organs.* This publication analyzes the practice by reference to individual provisions of the UN Charter. Another very useful research tool on the practice of the UN and its specialized agencies is the *United Nations Juridical Yearbook.* It reproduces, *inter alia,* important opinions rendered by the legal officers of the UN and the specialized agencies, summaries of the decisions of the UN and ILO Administrative Tribunals and of national tribunals bearing on the work of the UN, as well as selected resolutions and other legally significant information. Each volume also contains a useful systematic bibliography.

Although not designed for lawyers as such, the *Yearbook of the United Nations,* which chronicles the activities of the UN on an annual basis, is a most useful research tool. It provides the reader with a thorough overview of the work of individual UN organs, together with often hard to find citations to the relevant documents bearing on the subject under consideration. The *Annual Report of the UN Secretary-General* performs a similar function by summarizing the activities of the different UN organs.

The resolutions of the UN General Assembly and the Security Council are issued in separate publications. The resolutions of the subsidiary organs of the UN can be found in the annual reports these bodies submit to their respective parent organs. These reports frequently contain much information of interest to the legal researcher.

VI. FURTHER REFERENCE WORKS

§ 10–13. Additional help. Most American guides to legal research also contain sections on international law. See, for example, the very fine chapter on this subject in M. Cohen and R. Berring, *How to Find the Law* 838 (8th ed. 1983). This book provides excellent research guidance on the practice of, *inter alia,* the UN, the specialized agencies and the principal regional organizations. The following works are also very helpful:

J. M. Jacobstein and R. Mersky, *Fundamentals of Legal Research* (3d ed. 1987).

Sprudzs, "International Legal Research: An Infinite Paper Chase," 16 Vand.J.Transl.L. 521 (1983).

Williams, "Research Tips in International Law," 15 J. Int'l L. & Econ. 1 (1981) (and the useful bibliographic material compiled in the same issue, ibid., at 33 et seq.).

*

SUBJECT INDEX

AUTHOR INDEX

References are to Pages

273

AUTHOR INDEX
References are to Pages

†